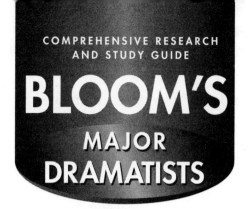

COMPREHENSIVE RESEARCH
AND STUDY GUIDE

# BLOOM'S
## MAJOR
## DRAMATISTS

*Arthur*
*Miller*

EDITED AND WITH AN
INTRODUCTION BY HAROLD BLOOM

# CURRENTLY AVAILABLE

## BLOOM'S MAJOR DRAMATISTS

Anton Chekhov
Henrik Ibsen
Arthur Miller
Eugene O'Neill
Shakespeare's Comedies
Shakespeare's Histories
Shakespeare's Romances
Shakespeare's Tragedies
George Bernard Shaw
Tennessee Williams

## BLOOM'S MAJOR NOVELISTS

Jane Austen
The Brontës
Willa Cather
Charles Dickens
William Faulkner
F. Scott Fitzgerald
Nathaniel Hawthorne
Ernest Hemingway
Toni Morrison
John Steinbeck
Mark Twain
Alice Walker

## BLOOM'S MAJOR SHORT STORY WRITERS

William Faulkner
F. Scott Fitzgerald
Ernest Hemingway
O. Henry
James Joyce
Herman Melville
Flannery O'Connor
Edgar Allan Poe
J. D. Salinger
John Steinbeck
Mark Twain
Eudora Welty

## BLOOM'S MAJOR WORLD POETS

Geoffrey Chaucer
Emily Dickinson
John Donne
T. S. Eliot
Robert Frost
Langston Hughes
John Milton
Edgar Allan Poe
Shakespeare's Poems & Sonnets
Alfred, Lord Tennyson
Walt Whitman
William Wordsworth

## BLOOM'S NOTES

The Adventures of Huckleberry Finn
Aeneid
The Age of Innocence
Animal Farm
The Autobiography of Malcolm X
The Awakening
Beloved
Beowulf
Billy Budd, Benito Cereno, & Bartleby the Scrivener
Brave New World
The Catcher in the Rye
Crime and Punishment
The Crucible

Death of a Salesman
A Farewell to Arms
Frankenstein
The Grapes of Wrath
Great Expectations
The Great Gatsby
Gulliver's Travels
Hamlet
Heart of Darkness & The Secret Sharer
Henry IV, Part One
I Know Why the Caged Bird Sings
Iliad
Inferno
Invisible Man
Jane Eyre
Julius Caesar

King Lear
Lord of the Flies
Macbeth
A Midsummer Night's Dream
Moby-Dick
Native Son
Nineteen Eighty-Four
Odyssey
Oedipus Plays
Of Mice and Men
The Old Man and the Sea
Othello
Paradise Lost
A Portrait of the Artist as a Young Man
The Portrait of a Lady

Pride and Prejudice
The Red Badge of Courage
Romeo and Juliet
The Scarlet Letter
Silas Marner
The Sound and the Fury
The Sun Also Rises
A Tale of Two Cities
Tess of the D'Urbervilles
Their Eyes Were Watching God
To Kill a Mockingbird
Uncle Tom's Cabin
Wuthering Heights

COMPREHENSIVE RESEARCH
AND STUDY GUIDE

# BLOOM'S
## MAJOR
## DRAMATISTS

# *Arthur*
# *Miller*

EDITED AND WITH AN INTRODUCTION
BY HAROLD BLOOM

3 5 7 9 8 6 4 2

Library of Congress Cataloging-in-Publication Data
Arthur Miller / edited and with an introduction by Harold Bloom.
    cm. — (Bloom's major dramatists)
Includes bibliographical references and index.
ISBN 0-7910-5246-X
1. Miller, Arthur, 1915-        —Examinations  Study guides.
I. Bloom, Harold.    II. Series.
PS3525.I515Z5142    1999
812'.52—dc21                                         99-26951
                                                    CIP

Chelsea House Publishers
1974 Sproul Road, Suite 400
Broomall, PA 19008-0914

The Chelsea House world wide web
address is www.chelseahouse.com

Contributing Editor: Pamela Loos

# Contents

# User's Guide

This volume is designed to present biographical, critical, and bibliographical information on the author's best-known or most important works. Following Harold Bloom's editor's note and introduction is a detailed biography of the author, discussing major life events and important literary accomplishments. A plot summary of each play follows, tracing significant themes, patterns, and motifs in the work.

A selection of critical extracts, derived from previously published material from leading critics, analyzes aspects of each play. The extracts consist of statements from the author, if available, early reviews of the work, and later evaluations up to the present. A bibliography of the author's writings (including a complete list of all works written, cowritten, edited, and translated), a list of additional books and articles on the author and his or her work, and an index of themes and ideas in the author's writings conclude the volume.

～

**Harold Bloom** is Sterling Professor of the Humanities at Yale University and Henry W. and Albert A. Berg Professor of English at the New York University Graduate School. He is the author of over 20 books and the editor of more than 30 anthologies of literary criticism.

Professor Bloom's works include *Shelley's Mythmaking* (1959), *The Visionary Company* (1961), *Blake's Apocalypse* (1963), *Yeats* (1970), *A Map of Misreading* (1975), *Kabbalah and Criticism* (1975), and *Agon: Toward a Theory of Revisionism* (1982). *The Anxiety of Influence* (1973) sets forth Professor Bloom's provocative theory of the literary relationships between the great writers and their predecessors. His most recent books include *The American Religion* (1992), *The Western Canon* (1994), *Omens of Millennium: The Gnosis of Angels, Dreams, and Resurrection* (1996), and *Shakespeare: The Invention of the Human* (1998), a finalist for the 1998 National Book Award.

Professor Bloom earned his Ph.D. from Yale University in 1955 and has served on the Yale faculty since then. He is a 1985 MacArthur Foundation Award recipient, served as the Charles Eliot Norton Professor of Poetry at Harvard University in 1987–88, and has received honorary degrees from the universities of Rome and Bologna. In 1999, Professor Bloom received the prestigious American Academy of Arts and Letters Gold Medal for Criticism.

Currently, Harold Bloom is the editor of numerous Chelsea House volumes of literary criticism, including the series BLOOM'S NOTES, BLOOM'S MAJOR SHORT STORY WRITERS, BLOOM'S MAJOR POETS, MAJOR LITERARY CHARACTERS, MODERN CRITICAL VIEWS, MODERN CRITICAL INTERPRETATIONS, and WOMEN WRITERS OF ENGLISH AND THEIR WORKS.

# Editor's Note

As there are more than two dozen Critical Views extracted here, I will confine myself to a few remarks upon observations that have influenced me. Miller himself is always provocative when reflecting upon his own work, and is joined here by the distinguished critic Eric Bentley.

I find very useful the attempts of several of the critics to invoke tragic tradition, from *Oedipus* onwards, in order to center their consideration of Miller.

In general, Miller's exegetes are constrained by the manifest limits of his art. Their tendency to make sociological observations upon his work follows his own lead, but sometimes brings about the paradox that the largeness of the American social dilemma, the notorious "American Dream," tends to overcome the sharpness of Miller's critiques.

# Introduction

## HAROLD BLOOM

"A man can get anywhere in this country on the basis of being liked." Arthur Miller's remark, made in an interview, has a peculiar force in the context of American political and social history. One reflects upon Ronald Reagan, a President impossible (for me) either to admire or to dislike. Miller, despite his palpable literary and dramatic limitations, has a shrewd understanding of our country. *Death of Salesman* is now half a century old, and retains its apparently perpetual relevance. The American ethos is sufficiently caught up by the play so that Miller's masterwork is clearly not just a period piece, unlike *All My Sons* and *The Crucible*, popular as the latter continues to be.

Arthur Miller is an Ibsenite dramatist, though his Ibsen is mostly a social realist, and not the visionary of the great plays: *Peer Gynt, Brand, Hedda Gabler,* and *When We Dead Awaken.* That Ibsen is himself something of a troll: obsessed and daemonic. Imaginative energy of that order is not present in Miller, though *Death of a Salesman* has an energy of pathos very much its own, the entropic catastrophe that Freud (with some irony) called "Family Romances."

Family romances almost invariably are melodramatic; to convert them to tragedy, you need to be the Shakespeare of *King Lear,* or at least of *Coriolanus.* Miller has a fondness for comparing *Death of a Salesman* to *King Lear,* a contrast that itself is catastrophic for Miller's play. Ibsen, at his strongest, can sustain some limited comparison to aspects of Shakespeare, but Miller can not. Like Lear, Willy Loman needs and wants more familial love than anyone can receive, but there the likeness ends.

Does Miller, like Eugene O'Neill, write the plays of our moral climate, or have we deceived ourselves into overestimating both of these dramatists? American novelists and American poets have vastly surpassed American playwrights: there is no dramatic William Faulkner or Wallace Stevens to be acclaimed among us. It may be that day-to-day reality in the United States is so violent that stage drama scarcely can compete with the drama of common events and uncommon persons. A wilderness of pathos may be more fecund matter for storytellers and lyricists than it can be for those who would compose tragedies.

Perhaps that is why we value *Death of a Salesman* more highly than its actual achievement warrants. Even half a century back, an universal image of American fatherhood was very difficult to attain. Willy Loman moves us because he dies the death of a father, not of a salesman. Whether Miller's critique of the values of a capitalistic society is trenchant enough to be persuasive, I continue to doubt. But Loman's yearning for love remains poignant, if only because it destroys him. Miller's true gift is for rendering anguish, and his protagonist's anguish authentically touches upon the universal sorrow of failed fatherhood. ❀

# Biography of
# Arthur Miller

"All these years later when I see a play of mine that I wrote thirty-five years ago, and I see that the audience is screwed into it in the way that they were in the first place, I like to believe that the feeling that they have is that man is worth something. . . . I think art imputes value to human beings and if I did that it would be the most pleasant thought I could depart with. . . ." So stated Arthur Miller in an interview published in 1990. An unpretentious man, he creates characters with dignity and has defended the protection of human dignity in numerous venues aside from theater.

But the young Arthur initially was more concerned with being an athlete than an advocate. Born in Manhattan on October 17, 1915, he was the second of three for Isadore and Augusta Miller, a well-to-do Jewish couple. In 1929 the stock market crash and Depression forced his father out of the coat business and their family out of their home to a small frame house in Brooklyn. Upon graduating from Abraham Lincoln High School in 1932, Miller started saving as much as he could from his income at an auto-parts warehouse so he could go to college. He occasionally would read on the subway on his way to work, and when he happened upon *The Brothers Karamazov,* "all at once believed I was born to be a writer."

But when he applied to the University of Michigan, he was turned down until he tried for a third time with a convincing letter he sent to the admissions officer. Having heard the school gave writing prizes, he enrolled in journalism, and within eighteen months he began writing plays, winning the Avery Hopwood Award on his first try for a piece he had written in just four days, *Honors at Dawn.* He received another Hopwood for his second work, *No Villain,* just one year later in 1937.

After he received his B.A. in 1938, Miller went back to New York and worked with the Federal Theatre Project until it was abolished; he then ended up on welfare. He completed his play, *The Golden Years,* and to make money he wrote numerous radio scripts, work he hated. In 1940 Miller married Mary Grace Slattery, to whom he had become engaged at the University of Michigan; they moved to

Brooklyn and eventually had two children. He held various odd jobs and kept writing for the next four years, while she served as the main breadwinner, working as a waitress and editor.

In 1944, his first Broadway production took place. The play's title, *The Man Who Had All the Luck,* certainly wasn't applicable to Miller at the time, for the piece struggled through only six performances, although it managed to win the Theatre Guild National Award.

A back injury kept Miller out of the military, but he visited army camps during the war and published his journal, *Situation Normal,* in 1944. By 1945 Miller switched gears and wrote a novel, *Focus,* about anti-Semitism. He became increasingly involved in leftist organizations and liberal causes. Then in 1947 his first son was born, and his first successful Broadway play was produced, *All My Sons.* It showed the after-effects of World War II on a family whose father had sold faulty plane parts to the government.

But Miller's most famous play by far became *Death of a Salesman,* which centered on a dejected salesman's final days. It was composed in six weeks on a typewriter Miller had bought with the money he earned from his first Hopwood. That year, 1949, the Pulitzer Prize was awarded for the first time—to Miller. He also received the New York Drama Critics' Circle Award for the work, which continued through 1950 for 742 performances. The same year Miller traveled to California to work on a film project. He met Marilyn Monroe and they saw each other frequently for many weeks.

In 1951 Miller published an adaptation of Henrik Ibsen's *An Enemy of the People.* Political commitments took up much of Miller's time then, and in 1953 he put his warnings about the dangers of mass hysteria and government power into the form of *The Crucible,* a work about the Salem witch trials that was readily construed as a metaphor for the McCarthy hearings then taking place.

By 1955 Miller's marriage was falling apart, and he met Monroe again at a theater party. They were seen together more and more, and he was divorced that year.

*The Crucible* was well-received, but it helped bring Miller negative attention of another sort. In June of 1956 he was subpoenaed to come before the House Un-American Activities Committee. Curiously, in the midst of his political troubles, he announced that he and Monroe had been secretly married. Before the Committee, Miller freely admitted his past associations with leftist groups, stating they had ended in 1950. But he refused to be a "good citizen" who would identify other Communists.

During this time, in 1955, Miller saw his *A View from the Bridge* produced on a double bill with a short play, *A Memory of Two Mondays*. His screenplay for the 1961 film *The Misfits* was created for his wife, who starred in it with Clark Gable, but shortly thereafter in that same year, they were divorced. Also in that year, Miller's mother died at the age of eighty.

In 1962, Miller married the photographer Inge Morath, with whom he had two children and collaborated on several books, writing text to accompany her images. By 1964, Miller's *After the Fall* was produced, creating more controversy than any of his previous work. Many critics balked at what they construed to be an excessively autobiographical piece.

Miller covered the Nazi trials in Frankfurt for the *New York Herald Tribune* and then wrote *Incident at Vichy* (1965), a short play about Nazism and anti-Semitism in Vichy France. In the same year he traveled extensively in Europe to oversee productions of his various works.

In 1966 approximately seventeen million viewers saw *Death of a Saleman* on television, twenty times the number who had seen the play when it was on Broadway. A collection of short stories, *I Don't Need You Anymore* (1967) followed, and another play, *The Price* (1968).

He was a member of the Connecticut delegation to the fateful Democratic National Convention in 1972, and he continued to be politically active and speak out for his beliefs. In 1973 the comic *The Creation of the World and Other Business* was produced, followed by *The Archbishop's Ceiling* (1977) and *The American Clock* (1980).

In 1983 Miller directed *Death of a Salesman* in China. In 1984 *Up from Paradise* was published, followed by *Danger: Memory!* in 1986, and his autobiography, *Timebends: A Life*, in 1987. He continued to see his works published and produced not only in theater but also on television. In 1994 *Broken Glass* was published, and in 1996 a film version of *The Crucible* was released.

Miller continues to write in his Connecticut home. Dustin Hoffman, one of the most famous Willy Lomans, describes Miller in *Arthur Miller and Company* as "so articulate. He's this great story-teller. He sounds like this New York cab driver; he's so unpretentious and earthy. You're laughing one minute, then you're thinking the next, and touched the next." ❀

# Plot Summary of
## *All My Sons*

*All My Sons* was not just Miller's second play but his second—and almost last—chance. It followed on the heels of *The Man Who Had All the Luck,* a play that struggled through no more than six performances and received mostly poor reviews. The play's sad showing made Miller question his abilities, to the point where he wrote in his introduction to the *Collected Plays:* "I was turning thirty then, the author of perhaps a dozen plays, none of which I could truly believe were finished. I had written many scenes, but not a play. . . . The decision formed to write one more, and if it turned out to be unrealizable, I would go into another line of work." Fortunately, *All My Sons* was well-received, and Miller continued writing. He went on to earn his place as one of the greatest American dramatists.

The play opens in the Kellers' backyard, in a small American town on a beautiful Sunday in August, just after World War II. It thematically discusses issues that appear again in Miller's following plays: humanity's responsibility to others, a father's conflict with his offspring, the human need for integrity, and the power of humanity's own self-destructive forces.

In the play's beginning, a small apple tree has blown over in the foreground. Joe Keller, the nearly-sixty-year-old self-made man, is reading the newspaper with his neighbor, the young, successful doctor Jim Bayliss. Other neighbors join them and take up easy conversation. Frank Lubey, a thirtyish neighbor, comments about the fallen tree and what a shame it is that it's been destroyed, since it was a memorial to Larry, Keller's son. Various neighbors ask about Annie Deever, the beautiful girl who grew up with her family in what is now the Baylisses' house, who has just arrived at the Kellers' the night before.

Keller's son Chris enters. His father asks him where Annie is and what he thinks his mother will say about the ruined tree. Chris reveals that his mother already saw the tree, since he heard it crack at about 4:00 A.M. and looked out the window, only to see her standing right next to it. He could hear her afterward crying in the kitchen. Joe asks quietly if she was crying very hard.

Chris says they've "made a terrible mistake" by letting his mother continue to believe that they, too, think that Larry is coming back after three years. Joe Keller is frightened at the thought of confronting her.

Chris tells his father that he asked Annie to come because he wants to marry her. But he is concerned about what Mother will say, for she believes Annie is still Larry's girl. Joe Keller asks him to think about the marriage further, since Chris hasn't seen Annie in five years. But Chris is insistent, sick of being a "good son too long, a good sucker." When he says that he will move away with Annie if he has to, his father is dumbfounded. Joe's dream is to have his son carry on his business, even though Chris says it doesn't inspire him. Joe cries, "What the hell did I work for? That's only for you, Chris, the whole shootin'-match is for you!" Chris says he needs his father's help if he is to stay. Joe puts his fist up to his son's jaw, but Chris is unflinching, and Joe backs down.

Kate Keller enters, preoccupied and somewhat distressed. She relates the dream she had about Larry that woke her up and made her go outside just as the tree broke. She remarks that they planted the tree for him too soon. "Too soon!" Chris exclaims. He argues that they need to forget about Larry.

Annie enters. Kate is genuinely overcome by her dress, but then, as if to downplay her own and her son's admiration, she asks Annie if she hasn't gained a little weight. Kate is eager to talk to Annie, and the men make fun, while Annie encourages Kate to ignore them. Kate tells Annie that she knows that deep in her heart Annie is still waiting for Larry. But Annie denies it and asks why Kate, in her own heart, feels he must be alive. When Kate tries to explain, Annie trembles, but still disagrees with Kate.

Frank appears and breaks the tension; he is taken by Annie. He says he's heard that her brother has gotten his degree. But then he asks about her father. This is the first that we learn that her father, Steve Deever, had worked with Joe but is now in prison. We also hear that Joe was exonerated from the charges that were brought against himself and Steve. All on stage are ill at ease until Frank leaves.

Annie explains that while at first she pitied her father, she then realized that he knowingly shipped out defective airplane parts; Larry's plane could have been one that crashed as a result. But Kate and Joe are insistent that this had nothing to do with Larry, since they all know Larry didn't fly a P-40. Joe also explains that the men in the factory were under pressure to produce the parts as fast as possible. He explains that Steve Deever was afraid, covered the cracks in the parts, and believed they would "hold up a hundred percent. That's a mistake, but it ain't murder." But Annie and Chris are unmoved. Chris nervously asks them to stop discussing the matter, and they agree, for the sake of happiness, to focus on the night's special dinner.

Chris and Annie are left alone, and the two reveal their love for each other. Annie admits that she almost got married two years ago, but she didn't when Chris started writing to her. Chris relates his experience as a commander of a company where almost all of the men were killed. He talks about the ability of these men to fight not only for their country but for each other, to selflessly do whatever the other men needed. He contrasts this to the world he sees now— selfish and focused on making money. Annie quiets his concerns. Her brother George calls from Columbus, the city where their father is, to say he is coming to the Kellers' on the next flight.

**Act II** opens with Chris sawing off the broken tree, leaving just the stump. George arrives, angry, wanting to take Annie away. He relates his father's side of the story: Steve Deever had telephoned Joe Keller when he saw the problem with the parts; Keller told him to cover the cracks in any way he could and ship them out. Steve was afraid; Keller said he was sick and couldn't come in, but he would take full responsibility for the decision. Chris doesn't believe the story and asks why George suddenly doesn't believe in Joe Keller's innocence. George says he had believed in Joe Keller all along—because Chris did.

There is a new mood when Kate enters. She cups "Georgie's" face in her hands, smothering him with motherly affection, and gets him to relax somewhat. Joe enters, and the pressure returns. He asks how Steve is, offers to give him a job when he's out of jail, and gives George examples of other times when his father failed to take responsibility for his actions. The atmosphere relaxes somewhat, until a seemingly innocent comment makes George realize that Joe Keller wasn't really sick on the day when his father called him for advice about the parts. George leaves in a rage. Annie will not leave with him, although Kate has already packed the woman's bags. Kate insists again that Annie is Larry's girl; she tells Chris that if Larry is dead, "your father killed him."

With this statement, Chris screams at his father: "Explain it to me or I'll tear you to pieces!" Joe tries to explain that if the parts hadn't been shipped, they would have lost the government business, and the factory would have collapsed, leaving him with nothing for his family. Chris burns with fury: "Is that as far as your mind can see, the business? . . . Don't you have a country? . . . What the hell are you? You're not even an animal, no animal kills his own, what are you?" He beats his fist on his father's shoulder until Joe stumbles away, weeping.

**Act III** opens at 2:00 A.M. the following morning. Chris has left. Annie begs Kate to admit to Chris that Larry truly is dead. She feels forced to show Kate a letter from Larry that apparently proves this. Chris returns, distraught and sick with himself for having done nothing before about his suspicions about his father. He says he will now be practical and just go away. "Do I raise the dead when I put him behind bars?" he asks. "What sense does that make? This is a zoo, a zoo!"

Annie grabs the letter from Kate and gives it to Chris to read. Larry wrote it on the day he died, telling Annie that he can't bear to live after seeing all of the newspapers relating what their fathers have done. He is going out on a mission in a few minutes, he writes, and he will probably never return; she shouldn't wait for him.

Joe says he is ready to go to jail. He admits that the soldiers who died because of their faulty airplane parts were "all my sons." He goes inside to get ready; a shot is heard from the house. Joe is dead. ❈

# List of Characters in
## *All My Sons*

**Joe Keller** is a heavy man, nearly sixty. A traditional, uneducated, small-town businessman for many years, he runs a factory that he expects his son to take over. He reminds the audience repeatedly that one's family always comes first; if it doesn't, he says, he would take a bullet to his head.

**Kate Keller** is his wife, in many ways a female version of her husband. A strong woman, she stands steadfastly behind her family, especially her husband. She is the only one who still believes that her son Larry, who is missing in action in World War II, is still alive.

**Chris Keller** is their idealistic son, thirty-two years old and solidly built. He recently returned from the war and is now an executive in his father's plant. But he is now somewhat disillusioned by the fact that civilians seem to have continued on in their concern with making money, nearly forgetting those who risked their lives for them. He thinks back to the selfless men that were in his unit.

**Ann Deever** is a little younger than Chris. She is the daughter of Joe Keller's now-imprisoned co-worker and the fiancée of the missing Larry. Now she is in love with Chris.

**George Deever,** Ann's brother, nostalgically recalls living in the neighborhood with the Kellers, but he disrupts the family with startling insinuations. He is a lawyer in his early thirties.

**Dr. Jim Bayliss** is a neighbor of the Kellers. Prompted by Chris Keller's idealism, he considers giving up his wealthy patients and returning to his true, but less well-paying, love—medical research.

**Sue Bayliss** is his wife, a heavy woman, near forty. She is annoyed that Chris Keller would put silly thoughts in her husband's head. She was once the object of George Deever's affections.

**Frank Lubey** is a pleasant, balding, low-key, thirty-two-year-old neighbor. Interested in astrology, he has promised Kate Keller he will do astrological research about the day Larry's plane went down.

**Lydia Lubey** is Frank's cheerful twenty-seven-year-old wife; they have three children. ❁

# Critical Views on
## *All My Sons*

ARTHUR MILLER ON JOE KELLER'S TROUBLE

[This extract, which initially appeared in the first volume of
Miller's *Collected Plays,* was written 10 years after the play
was first produced. In it Miller explains that the real
problem for Joe Keller is his belief that he is unconnected
from the world.]

It occurred to me that I must write this play so that even the actual
criminal, on reading it, would have to say that it was true and sensible
and as real as his life. It began to seem to me that what I had written
until then, as well as almost all the plays I had ever seen, had been
written for a theatrical performance, when they should have
been written as a kind of testimony whose relevance far surpassed
theatrics.

For these reasons the play begins in an atmosphere of undisturbed
normality. Its first act was later called slow, but it was designed to be
slow. It was made so that even boredom might threaten, so that
when the first intimation of the crime is dropped a genuine horror
might begin to move into the heart of the audience, a horror born of
the contrast between the placidity of the civilization on view and the
threat to it that a rage of conscience could create.

It took some two years to fashion this play, chiefly, I think now,
because of a difficulty not unconnected with a similar one in the
previous play. It was the question of relatedness. The crime in *All My
Sons* is not one that is about to be committed but one that has long
since been committed. There is no question of its consequences
being ameliorated by anything Chris Keller or his father can do; the
damage has been done irreparably. The stakes remaining are purely
the conscience of Joe Keller and its awakening to the evil he has
done, and the conscience of his son in the face of what he has discovered about his father. One could say that the problem was to
make a fact of morality, but it is more precise, I think, to say that the
structure of the play is designed to bring a man into the direct path
of the consequences he has wrought. In one sense, it was the same
problem of writing about David Beeves in the earlier play, for he too

could not relate himself to what he had done. In both plays the dramatic obsession, so to speak, was with the twofold nature of the individual—his own concept of his deeds, and what turns out to be the "real" description of them. *All My Sons* has often been called a moral play, and it is that, but the concept of morality is not quite as purely ethical as it has been made to appear, nor is it so in the plays that follow. That the deed of Joe Keller at issue in *All My Sons* is his having been the cause of the death of pilots in war obscures the other kind of morality in which the play is primarily interested. Morality is probably a faulty word to use in the connection, but what I was after was the wonder in the fact that consequences of actions are as real as the actions themselves, yet we rarely take them into consideration as we perform actions, and we cannot hope to do so fully when we must always act with only partial knowledge of consequences. Joe Keller's trouble, in a word, is not that he cannot tell right from wrong but that his cast of mind cannot admit that he personally, has any viable connection with his world, his universe, or his society.

—Arthur Miller, "Introduction to the *Collected Plays*" (1957). In *The Theater Essays of Arthur Miller,* ed. Robert A. Martin and Steven R. Centola (New York: Da Capo Press, 1996): pp. 129–131.

## SAMUEL A. YORKS ON JOE KELLER AND HIS SONS

[Samuel A. Yorks has taught English at Portland State College. Here he discusses what he sees as Miller's perspective on a major conflict in the play: Is the individual's loyalty to his family or the state?]

How does this opposition to the one-world view based upon abstract loyalty manifest itself within the play? Miller presents the strongest possible counter-statement. Joe Keller is above all loyal to his family—yet the dramatist presents him with insight and sympathy. Keller is consistently presented as "a man among men," and one capable of immense loyalty and affection. True, he is depicted as dodging responsibility at the time of the defective process in his plant by feigning illness and allowing his weaker partner to take the blame. But as he seeks to justify himself, Joe is allowed eloquence. He bitterly points out the profit motive that saturates the war effort: "Who worked for nothin' in that war? When they work for nothin', I'll work for nothin'. Did they ship a gun or a truck outa Detroit before they got their price? Is that clean? It's dollars and cents, nickels and dimes; war and peace, it's nickels and dimes, what's clean? Half the Goddamn country is gotta go if I go!" By his criticism of the national war effort Joe tries to obscure personal guilt but also points up the conflict of loyalties between the private clan and its extension, the state. Do all sacrifice equally for the total struggle or do some while others flourish? Is the abstract loyalty embodied in universal slogans really a monster feeding on the superior individual's finer sensibilities while pandering to the lusts of the callous and power oriented? Miller makes no obvious choice in *All My Sons* though he grants Joe Keller force and conviction. His cry lingers in our ears while we consider whether it is simple artistic integrity not to make of Joe a simple villain. Dramatic complexity is served in any event.

But the stature given Keller is only part of this contrary statement. What of mother Keller? Kate is easily the strongest individual in the play. She is shown as superior in force of character to all the others, especially in times of emotional crisis, except possibly when Anne presents for the first ⟨time⟩ Larry's letter. Kate affirms the most personal and private of loyalties; even when the letter destroys the family illusions her concern is for Joe rather than for herself. Mother Keller has dominated her husband by her knowledge of his actual guilt, but she subdues the hostile George Deever not by force but by the warmth of her response: "You offered it to him! *Give* it to him!" she exclaims to Anne Deever when she brings the grape juice to her brother. Kate Keller has for years protected her husband in crucial situations and has mastered others as well by her refusal to meet people on any level but that of the most direct, honest and personal. It is she who kept alive the myth that the lost son Larry would return. She does this to screen Joe, for if Larry is dead, then Joe killed him. This is not literally so, but in her mind Mrs. Keller connects Joe's guilty act with the absence of their son. And logic does not determine her thought; she is a creature of great emotion. Significantly, the most forceful and moving criticism of the war and its ideals is made by her as she rebuts the official views expressed by the rather sanctimonious Chris Keller. Referring to the pretty Lydia who married the zany Frank Lubey, mother Keller tells George Deever, "while you were getting mad about Fascism, Frank was getting into her bed." She also blasts the lofty ideals of the Eagle Scouts, as she terms George and her sons: "So now I got a tree." In addition to Larry's memorial, she laments Chris's bad feet and the aging George. One might again argue that this only demonstrates Miller's artistic control, for this woman's strong statement of a misguided personal loyalty only points the more vigorously the intensity and complexity of the struggle between opposed ideals. But possibly this strongly emotional language echoes what is close to its creator's heart. What adds potency to Kate's attack upon the ideals of embattled democracy is that her criticism is based upon love in contrast to the nickels-and-dimes economics of Joe Keller.

—Samuel A. Yorks, "Joe Keller and His Sons," *Western Humanities Review* 13, no. 4 (Autumn 1959): pp. 404–405.

## W. ARTHUR BOGGS ON *OEDIPUS* AND *ALL MY SONS*

[W. Arthur Boggs teaches at Slippery Rock University. His articles have appeared in various critical journals, and he has published more than two hundred poems. In this extract he supports his belief that *All My Sons* lacks tragic effect by comparing it to *Oedipus*.]

But in spite of Miller's ability as a dramatist, his treatment of Joe Keller and his problem does not result in superior, modern tragedy. As in *Oedipus*, at the beginning of the play we are not aware of the extent of Keller's guilt, nor of his own awareness of his guilt. As the play proceeds, we learn that Keller had been indicted for furnishing the army with cracked airplane engine blocks and then exonerated because the jury had believed that his partner, Steve Deever, was responsible. Much later in the play we learn that Keller actually was the guilty person but had craftily managed to shift the responsibility to his partner. At this point we also know that Keller had known of this phase of his guilt from the very beginning. But he several times denies that his crime had anything to do, and actually believes that it had nothing to do, with the death of his son, Larry, a World War II aviator. After all, Larry never flew the P-40 for which his father had made engine blocks. Larry could not have died as the direct result of his actions ⟨ ... ⟩

Having built up several strains of interdependent and complicated action, Miller is unable to resolve them in a satisfactory tragic climax. In order to convince Mrs. Keller that Larry is dead, Ann makes her read Larry's last letter, in which, having just received the news of the cracked engine blocks, he writes that he will fly away on the next day never to return. Over the protests of Mrs. Keller, Keller reads the letter, goes into the house, and commits suicide as he had said he would do if he were ever convinced that he was responsible for his son's death. Chris and his mother are left in the yard commiserating with each other.

For several reasons Miller's tragic muse fails him in this play. Although the social message of the play, one's responsibility to one's fellow man, can be a tragic theme, it seldom is. The tragic protagonist's dereliction from social responsibility normally places too much emphasis upon man in the mass rather than upon the outstanding individual who goes wrong. In developing several strains of action, Miller never clearly focuses his audience's attention upon his tragic protagonist, but keeps it jumping from the dead Larry to Mrs. Keller, to the romance between Chris and Ann, to the intervention of George, to the plight of Steve Deever, to several minor characters who intervene in the play for various reasons. Worst of all, Miller apparently never really decides upon his protagonist. Chris receives as much dramatic attention as his father; yet if *All My Sons* is a tragedy, it is the tragedy of Joe Keller, who has violated his social contract with humanity.

With dramatic material which could have led him to write a modern tragedy of recognition in which Joe Keller through a series of experiences was brought gradually to see himself for what he really is, Miller instead spreads his theme over several characters and brings his tragedy to a close by sudden revelation. Up to the last minutes of the play, Keller is convinced of his essential innocence in the one aspect of his crime which really matters to him, the death of his younger son. Convinced suddenly of his guilt, like Othello who suddenly discovers Desdemona innocent of all his suspicions, Keller takes his own life. If Miller attempted to write a modern tragedy of recognition like the *Oedipus,* he failed. In this failure lies much of the play's lack of tragic effect.

—W. Arthur Boggs, "*Oedipus* and *All My Sons,*" *The Personalist* 42, no. 4 (Autumn, October 1961): pp. 558, 559–560.

## ARVIN R. WELLS ON THE LIVING AND THE DEAD IN THE PLAY

[Arvin R. Wells is a former member of the English Department at Ohio University. He is the author of *Jesting Moses: A Study in Cabellian Comedy.* In this essay he points out that many have missed how *All My Sons* carefully covers the intricacies of motivation and relationships.]

Actually, like most of Miller's plays, *All My Sons* demands of the reader an awareness of the deviousness of human motivation, an understanding of the ways in which a man's best qualities may be involved in his worst actions and cheapest ideas, and, in general, a peculiarly fine perception of cause and effect. Nowhere is it suggested that the social realities and attitudes that are brought within the critical focus of the play can be honestly considered outside of some such context of human aspirations and weaknesses as is provided by the play; and nowhere is it suggested that the characters are or can be judged strictly on the basis of some simple social ethic or ideal that might be deduced from the action. The characters do not simply reflect the values and attitudes of a particular society; they use those values and attitudes in their attempt to realize themselves. And it is these characteristics that give *All My Sons,* and other Miller plays, a density of texture so much greater than that of the typical social thesis play, which seeks not only to direct but to facilitate ethical judgments upon matters of topical importance.

For most of us there is no difficulty in assenting to the abstract proposition which Chris puts to his mother at the end of the play:

You can be better! Once and for all you can know that the whole earth comes through those fences; there's a universe outside and you're responsible to it.

And there is no problem either in giving general intellectual assent to the morality of brotherhood for which Chris speaks. There is, however, considerable difficulty in assenting to the actual situation at the end of the play, in accepting it as a simple triumph of right over wrong. For the play in its entirety makes clear that Joe Keller has committed his crimes not out of cowardice, callousness, or pure self-interest, but out of a too-exclusive regard for real though limited values, and that Chris, the idealist, is far from acting disinterestedly as he harrows his father to repentance. ⟨ . . . ⟩

Because it forces upon the reader an awareness of the intricacies of human motivation and of human relationships, *All My Sons* leaves a dual impression: the action affirms the theme of the individual's responsibility to humanity, but, at the same time, it suggests that the standpoint of even so fine an ideal is not an altogether adequate one from which to evaluate human beings, and that a rigid idealism operating in the actual world of men entails suffering and waste, especially when the idealist is hagridden by his own ideals. There is no simple opposition here between those "who know" and those who "must learn," between those who possess the truth and those who have failed to grasp it, between the spiritually well and the spiritually sick. Moreover, the corruption and destruction of a man like Joe Keller, who is struggling to preserve what he conceives to be a just evaluation of himself in the eyes of his son, implies, in the context of the play, a deficiency not only in Keller's character but in the social environment in which he exists.

—Arvin R. Wells, "The Living and the Dead in *All My Sons*," *Modern Drama* 7, no. 1 (May 1964): pp. 46–47, 50–51.

## LEONARD MOSS ON MILLER'S NARRATIVE CRUDENESS

[Leonard Moss is a former professor of comparative literature at State University of New York College in Geneseo. Here he argues why the ending of *All My Sons* not only loses its focus on the main character but also dissipates tension.]

The narrative crudeness and verbal obscurity at the conclusion of *All My Sons* may be symptomatic of a shift in interest from the indignant father to the outraged son; after the last question spoken by Chris in the second act—"what must I do?"—Keller's defense no longer commands central attention. Miller seems to have become captivated by a figure recurrent in his work—a maturing individual (a New-man) who proclaims, in abstract terms, the interdependence of all men. The third act betrays a drift toward the rhetorical style Miller has called upon so freely elsewhere: sententious declarations delivered by Chris and by three colleagues in disenchantment differ radically in style both from the simple-minded banter prominent in the first act and from the intense exclamation and interrogation prominent in the second. ⟨ . . . ⟩

These moralistic speeches place a disproportionate emphasis on the antagonist's position, a change in focus that may account for the inconclusiveness of Keller's pre-suicide statement, with its token acquiescence in Chris's theory. Besides disrupting the development of the main character, moreover, such judgments dissipate tension. They produce an effect opposite to that achieved early in the play by the judicious alternation of serious and comic moods. After the cleanly decisive second-act clash between father and son, Chris's cynical wisdom comes as a wordy letdown: "we used to shoot a man who acted like a dog, but honor was real there, you were protecting something. But here? This is the land of the great big dogs, you don't love a man here, you eat him! That's the principle; the only one we live by—it just happened to kill a few people this time, that's all. The world's that way, how can I take it out on him? What sense does that make? This is a zoo, a zoo!" (Act III). (Similarly, Sue's long, misleading, and irrelevant criticism of Chris unduly slows the pace after the suspenseful conclusion of the first act.)

The playwright probably directed attention away from the father's loss to the son's in order to show the consequences of a thoroughgoing tribal outlook; "the fortress which *All My Sons* lays siege to," Miller stated, "is the fortress of unrelatedness." But in taking that course he undercut the source of emotional power he had cultivated during most of the play. *All My Sons,* for two acts an extremely well constructed work, reveals clearly what is evident in almost every play Miller has written—the habit of following a carefully prepared movement to crisis with an anticlimactic denouement. His desire to formulate "social" truths has restricted his talent for capturing inward urgencies in colloquial language.

—Leonard Moss, *Arthur Miller* (New York: Twayne, 1967): pp. 42–43.

## ROBERT W. CORRIGAN ON THE ACHIEVEMENT OF ARTHUR MILLER

[Robert W. Corrigan is President/Chancellor of San Francisco State University. He was the founder and first editor of *The Tulane Drama Review*. He is the author of *The Making of Theatre: From Drama to Performance* and *The World of the Theatre*. In his criticism that follows he describes how Miller's early plays have main characters that experience an identity crisis and break their connection with society.]

The central conflict in all of the plays in Miller's first period (*The Man Who Had All the Luck*—1944, *All My Sons*—1947, *Death of a Salesman*—1949, *An Enemy of the People*—1950, *The Crucible*—1953, *A Memory of Two Mondays*—1955, *A View from the Bridge*—1955, *A View from the Bridge*—1957) grows out of a crisis of identity. Each of the protagonists in these plays is suddenly confronted with a situation which he is incapable of meeting and which eventually puts his "name" in jeopardy. In the ensuing struggle it becomes clear that he does not know what his name really is; finally, his inability to answer the question "Who am I?" produces calamity and his ultimate downfall. Strange as it may sound, Joe Keller, Willy Loman, John Proctor, and Eddie Carbone are alike, caught up in a problem of identity that is normally characteristic of youth (one is almost tempted to say adolescence), and their deaths are caused by their lack of self-understanding. In every case this blindness is in large measure due to their failure to have resolved the question of identity at an earlier and more appropriate time in life. Miller presents this crisis as a conflict between the uncomprehending self and a solid social or economic structure—the family, the community, the system. The drama emerges either when the protagonist breaks his connection with society or when unexpected pressures reveal that such a connection has in fact never even existed. Miller sees the need for such a connection as absolute, and the failure to achieve and/or maintain it is bound to result in catastrophe. He makes this very clear in his introduction to *The Collected Plays*, where he writes about *All My Sons* as follows:

> Joe Keller's trouble, in a word, is not that he cannot tell right from wrong, but that his cast of mind cannot admit that he, personally, has any viable connection with his world, his universe, or his society. ⟨ . . . ⟩

Each of the plays written prior to *The Misfits* is a judgment of a man's failure to maintain a viable connection with his surrounding world because he does not know himself. The verdict is always guilty, and it is a verdict based upon Miller's belief that if each man faced up to the truth about himself, he could be fulfilled as an individual and still live within the restrictions of society. But while Miller's judgments are absolute, they are also exceedingly complex. There is no doubt that he finally stands four-square on the side of the community, but until the moment when justice must be served, his sympathies are for the most part directed toward those ordinary little men who never discovered who they really were.

A Miller protagonist belongs to a strange breed. In every instance he is unimaginative, inarticulate (as with Buechner's Woyzeck, the words that would save him seem always to be just beyond his grasp) and physically nondescript, if not downright unattractive. His roles as husband and father (or father-surrogate) are of paramount importance to him, and yet he fails miserably in both. He wants to love and be loved, but he is incapable of either giving or receiving love. And he is haunted by aspirations toward a joy in life that his humdrum spirit is quite unable to realize. Yet, in spite of all these negative characteristics, Miller's protagonists do engage our imagination and win our sympathies. I think this ambiguity stems from the fact that his own attitude towards his creations is so contradictory.

—Robert W. Corrigan, *Arthur Miller: A Collection of Critical Essays* (Englewood Cliffs, N.J.: Prentice-Hall, 1969): pp. 2–4.

[Barry Gross is a professor of English at Michigan State University and has also taught in Israel, England, Portugal, Turkey, and other countries. He has written books on F. Scott Fitzgerald. In this extract he questions why Miller doesn't bring Chris Keller to a clear awakening and have him create a noble plan for the future.]

In *All My Sons* Miller is not guilty of presuming to teach, or even of presuming to preach, but of not doing it with sufficient force and directness, of not pinpointing with sufficient sharpness Chris' amorphous and formless sentiments. *That* the world should be reordered is not at issue; *how* it should is.

"Where the son stands," Miller says in "The Shadow of the Gods," "is where the world should begin," but this does not happen in *All My Sons* anymore than it does in the "adolescent" plays Miller criticizes. It is undeniably true that "the struggle for mastery—for the freedom of manhood . . . as opposed to the servility of childhood—is the struggle not only to overthrow authority but to reconstitute it anew," but by this token Chris has achieved neither mastery nor manhood by the play's end. It might be argued that it is only after the play ends that Chris is equipped to make the world begin, to reconstitute authority anew, that is, only after he learns that his brother killed himself and watches his father do the same thing. If so, that is a high price in human life—to Miller, perhaps because he is not Christian, the highest price imaginable—to rouse Chris Keller to action. And, judging from Chris' past record, one cannot be sure that these two deaths will have that effect. The deaths of his comrades presented him with that opportunity before the play began and he has done nothing to reconstitute authority in their name. If we are to take Chris' stated sentiments about the men who died so that he might live seriously, then he is in the position at the beginning of *All My Sons* that Miller (in the *Sunday Times Magazine* article "Our Guilt for the World's Evil") sees the Jewish psychiatrist in at the end of *Incident at Vichy*: his is "the guilt of surviving his benefactors" and whether he is "a 'good' man for accepting his life in this way, or a 'bad' one, will depend on what he makes of his guilt, of his having survived." By that criterion, Chris Keller is a bad man when *All My Sons* begins and he is no better when the play ends.

Am I arraigning Miller unfairly? Am I asking more of his play than it need do or is supposed to do? Is not Miller entitled to exclude Chris Keller's vision of the future as well as Joe Keller's past in order to pinpoint the particular crime Joe is being prosecuted for? I think not. Our full awareness of that crime and our willingness to convict him of it is based on our belief that a better world is not only preferable but possible, that it not only should be made but could be made. Joe Keller's failure to find a connection with the world is a crime only if there is a world to connect with and only if there is a way to connect with it. ⟨ . . . ⟩

Chris should not be at such a loss to know how to reconstitute authority anew. If, as he complains, nothing changed at home, and if, as he says, it is a moral imperative for those who have survived to return home to change things, he should know what kind of changes should be made and how they might be accomplished.

> —Barry Gross, "*All My Sons* and the Larger Context," *Modern Drama* 18, no. 1 (March 1975): pp. 24–25.

## N. Bhaskara Panikkar on Morality and Social Happiness in Miller's Work

[N. Bhaskara Panikkar started teaching in 1960. He has been a lecturer in English in the Institute of Correspondence Courses at the University of Kerala, Trivandrum, India. He has published a number of articles and essays on American and Indian literature. While others have criticized Miller for presenting a confused morality in *All My Sons*, Panikkar supports Miller, explaining that man's moral nature is, in fact, paradoxical.]

Miller appears to hold the view that moral tension in the individual is natural and inevitable because moral absoluteness is inconceivable in the modern world. He is convinced that man is at once a mixture of good and evil, and that moralizers can at the same time be morality-breakers. ⟨ . . . ⟩ On the other hand, he believes in the possibility that human beings can at the same time be good and evil.

They can simultaneously distinguish evil and dedicate themselves to it and appear agreeable and normal. Miller thus sees man's moral nature as paradoxical. His heroes are therefore men of dual moral nature having the elements of both virtue and vice. The ensuing conflict in their personal moral approach creates moral tension. ⟨ . . . ⟩

Divergent moral responses to the same incident and to the same person are recurring traits in the character of Miller's heroes. Joe Keller, in *All My Sons*, deceives his partner, Steve Deever, and sends him to prison. With the help of "a court paper in [his] pocket to prove [he] wasn't" the criminal, he escaped punishment and "walked . . . past . . . the porches" of the court as a free man. Like an adept American racketeer, he knows that a phone call by which he has given orders to sell cracked airplane cylinder heads cannot be proved in a court of law. The result of this cunning contrivance is that he has become rich and big and has been "a respected man again". Thus far, from his actions it is reasonable to conclude that he is evil beyond redemption. But the actual Keller is not so. He is not that type of man who from start to finish is vicious and vicious alone. On the contrary, he is essentially good and innocent and he is evil because he is madly in love with the success dream which has been denied to him for a long time. In other words, it is his frustrated goodness, his frustrated love, that has made him evil. He is conscious of his crime and feels himself as "guilty as hell." His moral tension consequent on his guilty feeling is seen in his attempt to justify to Ann his deed. ⟨ . . . ⟩

Joe Keller's moral attitude at the time of his criminal deed and afterwards shows that his personal morality is self-contradictory. This is almost true of Chris's morality, too. When Chris discovers the complexity of his father's crime, he becomes so infuriated as to call his father an animal and to tear the tongue out of his father's mouth. But soon he retraces his steps from any such sin of patricide and hides behind the harmless philosophy that even by putting his father behind bars he cannot raise the dead. No loving son can take vengeance upon his father and no act of revenge compensates dead loss. But when an acclaimed moralist such as Chris hesitates to condemn an admitted crime, we begin to suspect his moral stance and stability. Hearing his father's sermon that half the goddam country has to go to jail if he goes, Chris wavers and reverses his earlier moral stand. He exonerates his father with a contradictory note that Joe Keller is "no worse than most men."

—N. Bhaskara Panikkar, *Individual Morality and Social Happiness in Arthur Miller* (New Delhi: Milind Publications, 1982): pp. 56–60.

## CHARLOTTE GOODMAN ON LILLIAN HELLMAN'S INFLUENCE ON MILLER

[Charlotte Goodman is a professor of English at Skidmore College. She has written about many twentieth-century female authors. Here she explains why, even more than Ibsen's work, Hellman's *Little Foxes* was the basis for *All My Sons*.]

There is, unfortunately, no personal testimony from Miller about Hellman's influence on his own plays. Nevertheless, I believe the striking parallels between his work and Hellman's suggest that she was an important if unacknowledged precursor. Although one might also fruitfully compare Hellman's *The Children's Hour* and Miller's *The Crucible*, I shall focus here on Hellman's *The Little Foxes* and Miller's *All My Sons*, two plays reminiscent of the social dramas of Ibsen. Both plays dramatize the sinful acts of parents and the coming of age of idealistic offspring who ultimately feel they must separate themselves from the tarnished world of their elders.

The protagonist of Hellman's *The Little Foxes*, Regina Giddens, and the protagonist of Miller's *All My Sons*, Joe Keller, are both preoccupied with money. In their efforts to acquire it, however, both commit misdeeds that their children cannot forgive. ⟨ . . . ⟩

Although Hellman and Miller expose the wrongdoings of their respective protagonists, they also want their audience to comprehend what motivated the unscrupulous behavior of these erring characters, for whom they appear to have had a great deal of sympathy. Dominating the respective plays in which they are found, neither Regina Giddens nor Joe Keller emerges as a one-dimensional villain of melodrama, despite their morally reprehensible behavior. 〈 . . . 〉

Miller, in *All My Sons,* also creates an erring protagonist with whose struggles we are nevertheless meant to empathize. Described as a "man among men," Joe Keller, like Regina Giddens, is preoccupied with money. Both the dependent Regina and the self-made businessman, Joe Keller, equate money with power, and both want to pass on to their children the power they themselves have struggled to attain. Echoing the comment Regina makes to her daughter, Joe Keller says plaintively to his son after he has uncovered the truth about Joe's criminal act, "Chris, I did it for you, it was a chance and I took it for you." In act 1, when Chris hints that he might want to leave the business, an alarmed Keller stammers, "Well . . . you don't want to think like that. . . . Because what the hell did I work for? That's only for you, Chris, the whole shootin' match is for you!" Most people would probably find Joe Keller a far more sympathetic figure than Regina Giddens, for he commits a crime outside the boundaries of family life, while Regina's crime directly involves her own family. As Hellman reveals, however, the patriarchal structure of the family denies Regina any access to power. In contrast to Regina, Joe Keller is able to create a power base for himself outside the family. When he is forced to behave unethically rather than risk a business failure, however, he too is willing to dirty his hands.

Not only are Regina and Joe parallel figures, but so are Alexandra and Chris. Both plays conclude with a dramatic confrontation between a parent and a child. The moral center of their respective plays.

—Charlotte Goodman, "The Fox's Cubs: Lillian Hellman, Arthur Miller, and Tennessee Williams." In *Modern American Drama: The Female Canon*, ed. June Schlueter (Rutherford. N.J.: Fairleigh Dickinson University Press, 1990): pp. 132, 133, 134.

## STEVEN R. CENTOLA ON THE PARADOX OF DENIAL IN *ALL MY SONS*

[Steven R. Centola is the founder and president of the Arthur Miller Society. He is professor of English at Millersville University in Pennsylvania and the author of *The Critical Response to Arthur Miller.* He has written and edited numerous works on Miller. In this essay he explains Miller's view that one's seemingly safe defense mechanism causes one's self-destruction.]

The play ends with Chris facing with horror his own complicity in his father's self-destruction, and with Keller's death the play force-fully repudiates anti-social behavior that derives from the myth of privatism in American society.

While one could discuss this central theme in *All My Sons* exclusively in terms of its social context and its call for socially responsible behavior, reducing the play and Miller's treatment of this issue to these terms alone fails to do justice to its complexity and fascinating exploration of universally significant questions about the enigmatic nature of the self's relation to others. For as Christopher Bigsby accurately observes, while *All My Sons* is a play about our ability to connect with others and the world around us, it is also about more than our success or failure at achieving such a connection:

> this is also a play about betrayal, about fathers and sons, about America, about self-deceit, about self-righteous-ness, about egotism presented as idealism, about a fear of mortality, about guilt, about domestic life as evasion, about the space between appearance and reality, about the suspect nature of language, about denial, about repression, about a kind of despair finessed into hope, about money, about an existence resistant to our needs, about a wish for innocence when, as Miller was later to say in his autobiography, innocence kills, about a need for completion, about the gulf between the times we live in and the people we wish to believe ourselves to be, about the fragility of what we take to be reality, about time as enemy and time as moral force and so on . . .

Ultimately, *All My Sons* is a play about both paradox and denial— or to state it more precisely, it is about a theme that Miller has described as "the paradox of denial." ⟨ . . . ⟩

Particularly because of his treatment of the theme of the paradox of denial, Miller's play has a resonance that transcends its contemporary society and immediate situation. The catastrophe that affects the Keller family can occur anytime so long as people choose to embrace a counterfeit innocence that conceals their impulse to betray and dominate others. *All My Sons* proves that Miller's later indictment of Germany during the Nuremberg Trials in *After the Fall* can just as easily apply to any country which fosters illusions that elevate the native populace above the ostensibly menacing and inferior foreigners. In a country at war with an external threat, perhaps it is especially easy to succumb to such self-deception, and in that case, then, the background to *All My Sons* makes the play's drama that much more salient and relevant. ⟨ . . . ⟩

In *All My Sons,* Miller shows how the impulse to betray and to deny responsibility for others, when left ungoverned, can run rampant and wreak havoc on the individual, his family, and his society—even, perhaps, civilization as a whole. The paradox of denial, therefore, is that the very defense mechanism that is employed to justify the rightness of a socially reprehensible act can ultimately become the exclusive means by which an individual self-destructs. The Kellers, and many of those around them, choose to blame everyone else for their dilemma, but only they are the authors of their destiny—and their failure to accept the tremendous burden of their freedom and responsibility is itself the cause of their personal tragedy.

—Steven R. Centola, "*All My Sons.*" In *The Cambridge Companion to Arthur Miller,* ed. Christopher Bigsby (Cambridge: Cambridge University Press, 1997): pp. 51, 58–59.

# Plot Summary of
## *Death of a Salesman*

There is a "need greater than hunger or sex or thirst, a need to leave a thumbprint somewhere on the world." Such were Arthur Miller's thoughts while conceiving *Death of a Salesman*. When the play was finished, it poignantly synthesized humanity's desire to undyingly chase a dream and become a success. The work was an immediate hit, and it earned Miller the Pulitzer Prize, as well as his own thumbprint on American literature. To this day the play is considered one of the great American classics.

While many critics speak of the play's concern with the American Dream, its themes are hardly limited to an American's understanding. The play takes issue with those who place too much emphasis on material gain, who devalue humanity, who believe success means pushing in front of everyone else. It jabs at people's concerns with the superficial. At the same time, the play harkens back to the "good old days," when refrigerators were made to last, there was room to breathe in your own backyard, and the people with whom you did business actually knew you.

The play's form also speaks out against convention. Miller recreates on stage what is going on in Willy Loman's mind; present and past mix, so that flashbacks actually become a part of the present action.

In the **first act**, Willy Loman, the exhausted "low man," enters with two very large suitcases. He tells his wife Linda that he had to turn around instead of finishing his sales trip, because he nearly had an accident while driving through Yonkers. He cannot concentrate, he admits, and we discover that this is not the first time this has happened. Linda says that he just needs a rest, and she offers that he ask his young boss if he can give up the traveling. At first incensed, Willy then succumbs to her idea and says he will talk to the boss in the morning.

The parents talk of their two sons, who are temporarily staying in their old rooms. Biff, the oldest son, has returned from out West for a visit. Willy complains about Biff being so lost and goes downstairs for a sandwich.

The boys hear their father talking to himself and get up from bed. Both are tall and handsome and unclear about what to do with themselves. Happy has the appearance of success; he works in a merchandising job and lives in his own apartment, but he is frustrated. He is a womanizer who says he cannot help himself. We find out later that he is an assistant to the assistant manager, and like his father, he lies to make himself sound better. He, too, has a limited view of what it means to be a success, to be "happy."

Biff speaks of his years of distress trying to work his way up in business. He is the idealist who cannot be confined by either the limitations of the business world's rules or the actual limitations of its buildings. He needs to be outside, in the expanse of the West, but his jobs out there haven't amounted to much. He plans to go back to the sporting goods store where he worked as a teenager; he wants to ask the owner, Bill Oliver, for a loan so he can buy a ranch.

We are brought back to Willy in the kitchen, who is still dreaming of the easy days when his boys were young. We see the insecure father who needs to impress his sons with exaggerations about the importance of his job. We see where his sons' restlessness and confused self-images come from. Then Willy confronts disturbing memories that get progressively worse. His voice gets loud enough to bring Biff downstairs to try to calm him, and it also brings out Charley, his friend from next door.

Charley's steadiness, patience, and practicality stand in stark contrast to the Lomans. He and Willy decide to play cards, but the game falls apart as Willy's mind conjures up his dead brother, Ben. Willy's conversation with Charley and Ben mixes together, until Charley gives up and leaves Willy to talk directly to Ben about his idea of success. Ben encapsulates the American dream and Willy's longings. Ben made millions in the diamond business in Africa in just four years and left his seven children the inheritance. Desperate for answers, Willy asks Ben "how he did it," but he gets no reply.

Willy has been so loud that all three family members from upstairs come down. He says he is going for a walk, and while he is gone, Linda candidly relates her worries. She knows that Willy has tried to kill himself by running his car into the railing of a bridge. He has also cut a hole in one of the gas pipes in the basement and attached a piece of rubber hose to it. Increasing his stress, his boss has put him on straight commission. Linda desperately appeals to the shocked men, especially Biff, for help. Biff agrees to stay home permanently and give them half of his paycheck. Willy returns and is strengthened by their hope.

In **Act II**, Willy goes to his young boss, Howard, and makes his pitch for a job that won't involve traveling. It doesn't matter to Howard that Willy worked with his father and gave Howard his name. Work is about money, and even though Willy says he will take less and less money if he doesn't have to travel, Howard tells Willy that not only can he not agree to this, but he cannot have Willy work for him at all right now.

Distraught, Willy goes to Charley's office and meets Bernard in the waiting area. Discussion turns to Biff; in typical Willy fashion, the salesman makes up a story about Biff's success. Then he stops and asks Bernard why Biff gave up on life. Bernard says he only knows that it happened not because Biff failed math but after a trip Biff made to meet Willy in Boston. Willy is notably disturbed and becomes defensive. Charley appears to see off his son, who, we hear, is going to argue a case before the Supreme Court. Willy is shocked that Charley hasn't bragged about this. Charley gives Willy the money he needs and begs him to take a job with him when he hears that Willy has lost his. But Willy, "on the verge of tears," says he cannot. "Charley," he says, "you're the only friend I got. Isn't that a remarkable thing?" But friends aren't enough in Willy's world.

The scene moves to a restaurant, where Biff tells Happy how foolish he was to even think that he could meet with Oliver, let alone get a loan from the man. He insists on telling Willy the truth when he gets there, but Willy makes it very hard by interrupting him with his hopeful questions and comments. Willy admits he was fired, and the discussion intensifies. "Don't you want to be anything?" Willy slams at his son. Eventually, when Willy realizes how bad the news is, he lapses into a flashback that mixes into the current conversation with his sons. We are taken back to the day when Biff met Willy in Boston, after the boy found he had flunked math. Willy remembers how Biff knocked over and over again on the hotel-room door, only to find his father inside with a half-naked woman. This, then, is what made Biff give up.

We go back to the family's kitchen, with the brothers and their mother late at night. Biff goes outside to Willy, interrupting his imaginary conversation with his brother Ben. Willy is telling Ben how well his wife and sons could do with twenty thousand dollars of life insurance money. Biff gets Willy to go inside, and the play rises to its peak. Biff insists on honesty; Willy accuses him of giving up on his life to spite his father. Biff says he must go, since his father will never see him for who he really is. Biff yells out, "Pop! I'm a dime a dozen, and so are you!" The line is in sharp contrast to the Lomans' typical, ever-positive external persona, but at the same time it is typically Lomanesque because it is so extreme.

Biff, exhausted, breaks into tears and collapses against his father, who is sitting in a kitchen chair. In a low voice, Willy asks why he is crying. When Biff gets up, Willy is "astonished, elevated" by the realization that his son "likes me!" Ironically, it gives him new incentive to continue with his plan. "That boy is going to be magnificent!" he proclaims. After the others go upstairs, he talks to Ben about his plan to kill himself, almost dancing at the wonderful life Biff will have as a result. Willy takes off in the car at full speed, driving to his death.

The final scene is at Willy's grave. Biff explains that Willy had all the wrong dreams and never really knew who he was. ❈

# List of Characters in
## *Death of a Salesman*

**Willy Loman** is a tired salesman in his sixties who continually grasps for the American Dream. Worn and weary from the quest, he still has an appealing intensity of spirit—a great drive to succeed, to have his kids succeed, and for all of them to be "well-liked." This same undaunted spirit, however, keeps Willy from accepting himself and his family for what they are, rendering him incapable of making any realistic, positive plans. Through the play, Willy spews language of self-reliance, self-confidence, and the smarts to excel, but we see that these are a cover for his own insecurities, confusion, fears of failing, and actual failings. Willy does have strengths: his steadiness in having worked hard enough for thirty-six years to pay off his mortgage, his compassion for his loving wife, and his devotion to his children that makes him teach them and genuinely try to inspire them. But Willy's insecurities overpower his strengths.

**Linda Loman** is Willy's ever-devoted wife. For her, Willy's needs are more important than her own and her sons. Linda is level-headed, with a clear perspective on the harsh realities of their situation, but when she talks to Willy she always does so with careful sensitivity so as not to upset him further. With her sons, however, Linda speaks frankly, rebuking them for their faults when they upset her husband. She reveals to her sons her husband's secrets that make it clear he has given up on life, and in desperation she appeals to Biff, her older son, to try to help Willy, since she seems unable to talk to him directly herself.

**Biff Loman** is Willy's favorite son. He is the oldest at thirty-four, a good-looking former athlete who was the promising star football player and who is now a troubled man. He suddenly gave up on life one summer when he decided not to take the summer classes he needed to graduate. He has drifted from job to job out West. He loves his father intensely and is disturbed at not being able to repair their relationship. He fights to be honest as he tries to get the family to confront reality.

**Happy** is the younger Loman son. He is like Biff in appearance, but he has lived a different life, with an apartment near home, working in business while also working his way through a slew of women. He throws out unconvincing comments about getting married and no one responds. While he wants his parents' approval and is genuinely fond of his brother, he rejects honesty. He is nearly the same at the beginning of the play as at the end, despite the tragedy that unravels in the household.

**Charley** is a neighbor and a generous friend of Willy's. His character is in striking contrast to Willy's, for Charley is sure and steady, calm and successful. He has no big dreams, but he does have a son to be proud of and his own good business to boast about—but he never does.

**Bernard** is Charley's son. In school, he was a studious, spectacled student who looked up to the athletic and magnetic Biff. He now has a wife and two sons, and he is a lawyer pleading a case before the Supreme Court. ❈

# Critical Views on
## *Death of a Salesman*

### ARTHUR MILLER'S COMMENTS ON THE PLAY'S
### ONE-YEAR ANNIVERSARY

[One year after *Death of a Salesman* opened, Arthur Miller reminded readers of the depth of audiences' imaginations and their need for hope.]

There are things learned—I think, by many people—from this production. Things which, if applied, can bring much vitality to our theatre.

There is no limit to the expansion of the audience's imagination so long as the play's internal logic is kept inviolate. It is not true that conventionalism is demanded. They will move with you anywhere, they will believe right into the moon so long as you believe who tell them this tale. We are at the beginning of many explosions of form. They are waiting for wonders.

A serious theme is entertaining to the extent that it is not trifled with, not cleverly angled, but met in head-on collision. They will not consent to suffer while the creators stand by with tongue in cheek. They have a way of knowing. Nobody can blame them.

And there have been certain disappointments, one above all. I am sorry the self-realization of the older son, Biff, is not a weightier counterbalance to Willy's disaster in the audience mind.

And certain things more clearly known, or so it seems now. We want to give of ourselves, and yet all we train for is to take, as though nothing less will keep the world at a safe distance. Every day we contradict our will to create, which is to give. The end of man is not security, but without security we are without the elementary condition of humaneness.

A time will come when they will look back at us astonished that we saw something holy in the competition for the means of existence. But already we are beginning to ask of the great man, not what has he got, but what has he done for the world. We ought to be struggling for a world in which it will be possible to lay blame. Only then will the great tragedies be written, for where no order is believed in, no order can be breached, and thus all disasters of man will strive vainly for moral meaning.

And what have such thoughts to do with this sort of reminiscence? Only that to me the tragedy of Willy Loman is that he gave his life, or sold it, in order to justify the waste of it. It is the tragedy of a man who did believe that he alone was not meeting the qualifications laid down for mankind by those clean-shaven frontiersmen who inhabit the peaks of broadcasting and advertising offices. From those forests of canned goods high up near the sky, he heard the thundering command to succeed as it ricocheted down the newspaper-lined canyons of his city, heard not a human voice, but a wind of a voice to which no human can reply in kind, except to stare into the mirror at a failure.

So what is there to feel on this anniversary? Hope, for I know now that the people want to listen. A little fear that they want to listen so badly. And an old insistence—sometimes difficult to summon, but there none the less—that we will find a way beyond fear of each other, beyond bellicosity, a way into our humanity.

> —Arthur Miller, "The 'Salesman' Has a Birthday," *The New York Times* (February 5, 1950), section 2, pp. 1, 3.

## George Kernodle on the Death of the Little Man

[George Kernodle has been an instructor of English and dramatic arts at numerous universities. He has directed more than one hundred plays and has translated and produced numerous Molière plays. He is the author of *Invitation to the Theatre* (1967, 1971) and other works. In this extract Kernodle argues that while tragedy traditionally cannot focus on the ordinary man, *Death of a Salesman* still works.]

So, we reach *Death of a Salesman*, a tragic study of a little man and his dream. Miller sets out to write a tragedy, well aware that tragedy is a high and noble thing, a thing of dignity and importance. He wrote a preface called "Tragedy and the Common Man," defending the possibility of a tragedy that has no kings or princes. What a long way we have come since the 1920's. The Little Man of that decade, sometimes presented as pathetic, could never have seemed important enough to be dignified by tragedy. Joseph Wood Krutch in 1929 in a famous chapter called "The Death of a Value," denied that our cynical age could believe that any man could be important enough to be the subject of a tragedy.

Miller goes straight to what has been the central problem of the modern man in a city—a vision of himself and his place in the world. The tragic quality, Miller writes, "derives from the underlying fear of being displaced, the disaster inherent in being torn away from our chosen image of what and who we are in this world. Among us today this fear is as strong, and perhaps stronger, than it ever was. In fact, it is the common man who knows this fear best." The key word for all the little men and Miller is "*indignity.*"

Miller rejects both the purely psychiatric view of life and the purely sociological. If all our miseries, our indignities, are born and bred within our minds, then all action, let alone the heroic action, is obviously impossible. On the other hand, if society alone is to blame, then there can be no validity to the character of the protagonist.

*Death of a Salesman* is a play that strikes a balance, a play that shows people facing economic and sociological questions but not a play to give neat answers—a play that looks at a dream from several different angles, no one of them final. Most important is the interaction of the inner dream and the outer world.

At least one critic has called Miller down severely for pulling his punches in his treatment of society. Why didn't he clearly come out and say that something is wrong with a business world that will fire Willy Loman so heartlessly after the years he had worked for the firm? But Miller was not writing a social problem play. For most of us it is all the stronger a play for concentrating on a complex character and letting the implications suggest what they may.

In the same way he is not completely explicit in saying that Willy's dream was all wrong. He does consider a dream all-important, and it does make a difference which dream a man has. But his main interest is in the grandeur and terror of a man who has had a great dream, and as he and society are changing feels that that dream is letting him down. His dogged devotion to that dream into the noisy jaws of death is in the pattern of the great tragedies. It does proclaim man's grandeur in his ability to live and die by his dream. The most important thing in a tragedy is not to analyze the sacred principle in detail but to sound the depth of the man when he has to face violating his sacred principle.

—George Kernodle, "The Death of the Little Man," *The Carleton Drama Review* 1, no. 2 (1955–56): pp. 56–57.

## GEORGE DE SCHWEINITZ ON EPIC AND TRAGEDY

[George de Schweinitz studied at Oxford and has taught at West Texas State College. In this extract, he outlines the three main sources of value in Willy Loman's America: American history and tradition, the frontier, and the city.]

At this point it will be necessary to turn back to the three main sources of value that the play posits as possible for—to use Miller's word—the "average" American of this age, that is, for the American who, like Willy, has what Miller calls "the common materials of life" to work with. American history and tradition is the first of these, the frontier the second, and the city the third and last.

Each of these three main sources of value is clearly objectified or particularized in *Death of a Salesman;* that is, each is given a "vehicle" or correlative in the total action and each shares objectively—or Realistically, to use Miller's term for this Ibsen-derived type of drama—in the total conflict leading to the catastrophe. To give their particular names, they are, first, New England, representing American history and tradition; second, Alaska and Africa, both frontiers in the sense of places ripe for economic development and exploitation; and third, New York, representing the city.

Let us take New England and examine its place in Willy's psychic as well as physical world. It is curious and significant that Willy, though late in life he is unable to make a living in New England, has nothing but good and kind thoughts about it. Earlier he had wanted to take the whole family there for a vacation. He never waxes rhapsodic about New York, but he does about New England. At times wistfulness and nostalgia come into his voice when he reminisces about New England. It has been the "field" that he has "ploughed"; it has yielded all the returns he has had for thirty years or more. It is "full of fine people" and "the cradle of the Revolution." To Willy, unlike New York, it is a place of historical significance in America; he even equates it with America. Instead of a geographical unit only, it is thus almost an essence to him, like the Pocahontas image, embodying an originally virginal and unspoiled America, in Hart Crane's *The Bridge.* Most important of all, it carries this high and imperishable image in Willy's mind; there old salesmen never die but only "fade away" to the hotel telephone where they carry on their extensive businesses amid increasing popularity and love. Willy's heartfelt description of the salesman over eighty who actually conducted business in this fashion suggests a worship of a state that appears as nothing less than the ideal. This is the salesman's Paradise. It may seem a tawdry one as Paradises go, but it may well be the best that a run-of-the-mill American salesman with headquarters in New York in the mid-twentieth century, can imagine.

—George de Schweinitz, "Death of a Salesman: A Note on Epic and Tragedy," Western Humanities Review 14, no. 1 (Winter 1960): pp. 93–94.

## Barry Gross on Willy as Peddler and Pioneer

[Barry Gross is a professor of English at Michigan State University and has also taught in Israel, England, Portugal, Turkey, and other countries. He has written books on F. Scott Fitzgerald. Here he shows why a man in Willy's America cannot be both peddler and pioneer, and discusses Willy's father.]

Although much has been written about *Death of a Salesman,* the use to which Arthur Miller has put the American frontier tradition—especially the motifs of peddler and pioneer—has not been sufficiently discussed.

First of all, Willy Loman thinks of himself as, in his own right, a pioneer:

> WILLY. When I went north the first time, the Wagner Company
> didn't know where New England was.

This characterization of Willy as pioneer is not sarcastic or ironic. It is consistent with the small scale of Willy's life that his frontier is not, say, the Northwest Territory but—quite literally, in the salesman's jargon—the New England Territory. However, such a frontier is not enough for Willy. He must try to create a literal one:

> WILLY. It's Brooklyn, I know, but we hunt too.
> BEN. Really, now.
> WILLY. Oh sure, there's snakes and rabbits and—that's why I
> moved out here. Why, Biff can fell any one of these trees in
> no time!

But why should it be necessary for Willy Loman, an easterner, in the nineteen-forties, to create a frontier in the backyards of Brooklyn? Why should he feel the need to be a pioneer? If the answer were only that Willy is an American and that the frontier is a significant force in the American consciousness, then the play would not be nearly so effective and Willy would not be nearly so moving. True, Willy Loman *is* a contemporary Everyman—or, at least, Everyamerican—but he must also be, at the same time, a particular human being, if *Death of a Salesman* is to be anything more than a dissection of a national disease. No, Willy Loman must need a frontier for particular, as well as universal, reasons.

The father-son relationship is one of the major motifs in *Death of a Salesman*. In addition to the most important relationship between Willy and his sons, there is neighbor Charley and his son Bernard, and Willy's dead boss Wagner and his son Howard. But it is too frequently forgotten that Willy, too, has a father. And it is his father, the exemplar of the Yankee peddler, who helps to explain, in large part, Willy's need for a frontier and to suggest some of the reasons for Willy's failure:

> BEN. Father was a very great and wild-hearted man. We would start
> in Boston, and he'd toss the whole family into the wagon,
> and then he'd drive the team right across the country;
> through Ohio, and Indiana, Michigan, Illinois, and all the

Western states. And we'd stop in the towns and sell the
flutes that he'd made on the way. Great inventor, Father.
With one gadget he made more in a week than a man like
you could make in a lifetime.

And it is certainly true that some of this spirit survives in Willy. He,
too, wanders a territory peddling wares. But they are not his own
wares made with his own hands. Nor can he choose his own territory: Willy has started and ended in Boston. The fault is not Willy's:
given the tradition in which he was raised, Willy Loman is simply in
the wrong place at the wrong time. A man can no longer wander the
country selling what he makes with his own hands. If a man is to be
peddler, he cannot, as his father was, be pioneer as well.

—Barry Gross, "Peddler and Pioneer in *Death of a Salesman*," *Modern
Drama* 7, no. 4 (Spring 1965): pp. 405–406.

## ALFRED R. FERGUSON ON THE TRAGEDY OF
## THE AMERICAN DREAM

[Alfred R. Ferguson has been an associate professor of
English at the University of Wisconsin in Oshkosh. He is
the author of essays that have appeared in numerous literary journals. Here he studies the different types of
dream sequences Willy experiences, showing how his
dreams about his family and its values point to his own
lack of moral direction.]

There is something different about success in America, different
from success elsewhere. "The very rich," said Fitzgerald to Hemingway in the famous anecdote, "are different from you and me." To
which Hemingway replied, "Yeah. They got more money." But Hemingway's sardonic wit to the contrary, there is something different.
The difference is the mythic opportunity afforded everyman. The
American Dream assures one and all the chance to strike it rich. Or
the chance for personal fulfillment if, like Jay Gatsby in Fitzgerald's
novel, riches are perceived as the threshold to paradise, not the key.

But how to transcend the distance between the front steps of Gatsby's mansion and that green light at the end of Daisy Buchanan's boat dock? What is the secret? After what good works, after what grace visited upon him does everyman walk into his backyard and, in the language of an extremely popular lecturer of the Guilded Age, find "acres of diamonds." If, as promised, believing in it and being willing to sacrifice anything for it make the American Dream come true, both Gatsby and Willy Loman should have entered the gates of paradise.

The many dream sequences of the play, so skillfully woven into the action by Miller's masterful stagecraft, are in fact historical "researches" by Willy, projections of the past into the present by Willy's acute historical recollection. They are hallucination, in that they are not self-willed, but not a classic illustration of clinical psychosis, wherein the mind withdraws from reality, or is detached from reality to the point of substituting fantasy for fact. The past Willy "hallucinates" has been actual and, central to the play's meaning, is active in the present: "dream rising out of reality." That is, the past has shaped the future, which is the present time in which the play's events take place. The past, or history, has not been transcended, as indeed it cannot be except in myth. And, also central to the play's meaning and to Willy as the personification of the American Dream, Willy though aware of the past is unaware of its real significance to the present. ⟨ . . . ⟩

The dream sequences fall into three categories. The first is in the general context of Willy's family, the primary purpose of which is to show the values Willy has communicated to his sons, Biff and Happy. The second dramatizes Biff's traumatic discovery of "The Woman" in his father's hotel room when he unexpectedly visits Willy in Boston. The third comprises the "visits" from Ben, Willy's older brother. These are real incidents from the past, until Ben's appearance at the end of the last act, when his presence is a hallucinatory projection of Willy's disoriented present. But Ben's "presence" in Willy's hallucination though imaginary is yet an empiric result or effect of the past.

The dream sequences involving Willy and his family dramatize his moral confusion and lack of direction. It is important for success, Willy says repeatedly to his sons, not only to be liked, but to be "well-liked." ⟨ . . . ⟩

Personal magnetism ("charisma" in contemporary jargon), making an impression, having contacts, being well liked make up the "secret" of success. But, curiously, Willy does not like himself. He knows, inchoately to be sure, yet he does know that there is no concrete foundation to his life, no definitive spiritual values or moral direction.

—Alfred R. Ferguson, "The Tragedy of the American Dream in *Death of a Salesman*," *Thought* 53, no. 208 (March 1978): pp. 90–91, 92.

## RICHARD T. BRUCHER ON TECHNOLOGY AND THE COMMON MAN

[Richard T. Brucher is a professor of English at the University of Maine, Orono. In this extract he compares Loman to Whitman, since both rant over technology destroying nature but also marvel at technology's power.]

As *Death of a Salesman* opens, Willy Loman returns home "tired to the death." Lost in reveries about the beautiful countryside and the past, he's been driving off the road; and now he wants a cheese sandwich. But Linda's suggestion that he try a new American-type cheese—"It's whipped"—irritates Willy: "Why do you get American when I like Swiss?" His anger at being contradicted unleashes an indictment of modern industrialized America:

> The street is lined with cars. There's not a breath of fresh
> air in the neighborhood. The grass don't grow anymore,
> you can't raise a carrot in the back yard.

In the old days, "This time of year it was lilac and wisteria." Now: "Smell the stink from that apartment house! And another one on the other side. . . ." But just as Willy defines the conflict between nature and industry, he pauses and simply wonders: "How can they whip cheese?"

The clash between the old agrarian ideal and capitalistic enterprise is well documented in the literature on *Death of a Salesman*, as is the spiritual shift from Thomas Jefferson to Andrew Carnegie to Dale Carnegie that the play reflects. The son of a pioneer inventor and the slave to broken machines, Willy Loman seems to epitomize the victim of modern technology. But his unexpected, marvelingly innocent question about whipping cheese reveals an ambivalence toward technology livelier and more interesting (and perhaps truer to the American character) than a simple dichotomy between farm and factory, past and present. *Death of a Salesman* engages an audience's conflicting attitudes toward technology: fear of the new and unfamiliar; marvel at progress; and the need, finally, to accommodate technology to cultural mythologies by subordinating it to personality. Willy's contradictions clearly indicate his alienation, but they recall Walt Whitman, too (the other restless Brooklynite who could sing enthusiastically of leaves of grass, lilacs, and locomotives in winter). "Do I contradict myself?" Whitman asks near the end of *Song of Myself;* "Very well then I contradict myself, / (I am large, I contain multitudes.)" ⟨ . . . ⟩

I do not claim the status of Whitman's divine poet for either Arthur Miller or Tracy Kidder, the author of *The Soul of a New Machine.* But both are fine connectors who invoke the spirit of Whitman, Thoreau, and Emerson as they help us integrate technology with cultural mythologies and thus triumph over it in the popular imagination. Indeed, the great American writers of the nineteenth century define, in part, the tradition into which some contemporary writers try to fit modern technological enterprise.

Miller endows Willy Loman with a Whitmanesque urge to appropriate technology to his personal vision, not just consume it. This quality complicates Willy's relationship with technology, and thus the whole notion of his pathetic victimization.

—Richard T. Brucher, "Willy Loman and *The Soul of a New Machine:* Technology and the Common Man," *Journal of American Studies* 17, no. 3 (December 1983): pp. 325–326.

## LEAH HADOMI ON FANTASY AND REALITY IN THE PLAY

[Leah Hadomi is a senior lecturer of Comparative Literature at Haifa University in Israel. She has written several articles on drama and on the postwar German novel and cinema. In the following criticism she explains the role of each of the men from Willy's past that he dreams about, and the roles of their parallel selves in Willy's current life.]

Willy is not content to admire these men. He also internalizes their qualities and the ideas they represent, diminishing and trivializing them in the process. Thus the ideas of being in close touch with nature and taking to the open road that are inspired by Willy's memory of his father are diminished in his own life to puttering about in the back yard of his suburban Brooklyn home and making his routine rounds as a traveling salesman; the idea of venturesome private enterprise for high stakes represented by his brother depreciates to drumming merchandise for a commission; and even the example of Singleman's being "remembered and loved and helped by so many different people," over which Willy rhapsodizes to Howard Wagner, is degraded in his own aspirations to the condition of being merely popular and well-liked.

Three of the characters among the principle *dramatis personae* of the play, Biff, Happy and Charley, function in the real world as analogous to the ideal types in Willy's consciousness. Though none of them is a complete substantiation of Willy's ego ideals, there is in each character a dominant trait that identifies him with either Willy's father, or Ben, or Dave Singleman, and that determines Willy's relationship to him.

—Leah Hadomi, "Fantasy and Reality: Dramatic Rhythm in *Death of a Salesman*," *Modern Drama* 31, no. 2 (June 1988): pp. 160–161.

## ARTHUR MILLER: THE AUDIENCE CAN'T ESCAPE

[This extract is taken from an interview of Miller by Christopher Bigsby, a professor of American Studies at the University of East Anglia and the director of the Arthur Miller Centre. Bigsby has written more than 20 books on theater and American culture. In this piece, published more than 40 years after *Death of a Salesman* was first produced, Miller explains how he held the audience captive.]

**Bigsby:** Do you ever feel, in looking back, that there is a kind of rift in *Death of a Salesman*, in that our dramatic attention is on Willy Loman but the play's moral resolution really turns on Biff's self-realisation? Is that why some people thought of the play as pessimistic, because they were looking in the wrong place?

**Miller:** Well, I'm sure that's why. There is a rift in it in that sense. You know, Thomas Mann saw that play, and he said, 'You know, the thing about the play is that it is a lyric play, but you never tell them what to think. It is simply an experience that they can't escape.' Now of course this is part of the reason that there's all this debate about the play. You see, I never allowed them to go beyond their intellectual and emotional capacity. There is no line in there that goes beyond what they could possibly have realised. The consequence is that, unlike standard tragedy, where you have the right, so to speak, formally speaking, to make self-aware statements where the character is aware of the play he is in, I never let them become aware of the play they are in. All that was driven out, ruthlessly, because at that time I resolved that I was going to make that audience never escape, even at the risk of losing objectivity, if I could do it. Because, I believed in squeezing out all the self-consciousness in the play. Every scene in that play begins late. There are no transitions in the play. It starts with a man who is tired. He doesn't get tired. He's tired in the first second of the play. You can tell from the way he enters the play. On the first line, she says, 'What happened?' Nothing happened but he's exhausted. You know you're somewhere. The same is true of every scene in that play. I completely drove out the usual transitional material from the play. That's the form of the play, that I never allowed into it the self-conscious statements, which Mann wisely recognised. ⟨ . . . ⟩

The audience knew what *Salesman* was about. They knew he wasn't crazy. They were right up with him. See, let me not underestimate it, I was ironically stating all the things that they always state seriously. A man can get anywhere in this country on the basis of being liked. Now this is serious advice, and that audience is sitting there almost about to smile but the tears are coming out of their eyes because they know that that is what they believe.

—Christopher Bigsby, *Arthur Miller and Company* (London: Methuen Drama, 1990): pp. 55–56, 58.

[Steven R. Centola is an associate professor of English at Millersville University. His work has appeared in the *Midwest Quarterly, Arizona Quarterly, South Atlantic Review,* and other journals. Here he explains that the powerful appeal of the play is its focus on Willy's gut-wrenching need to appraise himself and justify his life.]

Studies of Arthur Miller's *Death of a Salesman* invariably discuss Willy Loman's self-delusion and moral confusion in relation to Miller's indictment of the competitive, capitalistic society that is responsible for dehumanizing the individual and transforming the once promising agrarian American dream into an urban nightmare. While Miller clearly uses Willy's collapse to attack the false values of a venal American society, the play ultimately captures the audience's attention not because of its blistering attack on social injustice but because of its powerful portrayal of a timeless human dilemma. Simply put, Miller's play tells the story of a man who, on the verge of death, wants desperately to justify his life. As he struggles to fit the jagged pieces of his broken life together, Willy Loman discovers that to assuage his guilt, he must face the consequences of past choices and question the values inherent in the life he has constructed for himself and his family. Willy's painful struggle "to evaluate himself justly" is finally what grips the play's audiences around the world, for everyone, not just people who are culturally or ideologically predisposed to embrace the American dream, can understand the anguish that derives from "being torn away from our chosen image of what and who we are in this world." ⟨ . . . ⟩

Throughout the play, Willy exhibits several important personality traits. Thoroughly convinced that "the man who makes an appearance in the business world, the man who creates personal interest, is the man who gets ahead," Willy is ever conscious of his appearance before others. Quite literally, Willy is probably obsessed with personal appearance because, in his mind, he was convinced himself that since he is destined for success, he must constantly dress the part. However, such fastidiousness also betrays his insecurity, something which often surfaces in his contradictory statements and emotional outbursts—these, of course, being a constant embarrassment for his family as well as a painful reminder to Willy of his ridiculous appearance before others. Beneath the surface optimism, therefore, lurk his frustration and keen sense of failure. That is why he can be spry, amusing, and cheerful one moment and then suddenly become quarrelsome, insulting, and sullen the next. Through Willy's incongruous behavior, Miller makes us sharply aware of the subterranean tensions dividing Willy.

Perhaps just as important as this, though, is the realization that with all of his seemingly absurd antics, and with his humor, quick intelligence, and warmth, Willy becomes likable, if not well liked. Even if we disagree with his actions, we still understand his anguish, share his suffering, and even come to admire him for his relentless pursuit of his impossible dream. With Miller, we come to see Willy as "extraordinary in one sense at least—he is driven to commit what to him is a consummate act of love through which he can hand down his selfhood, his identity. Perversely, perhaps, this has a certain noble claim if only in his having totally believed, and dreamed himself to death."

—Steven R. Centola, "Family Values in *Death of a Salesman*," *CLA Journal* 37, no. 1 (September 1993): pp. 29–31.

# Plot Summary of
## *The Crucible*

Disturbingly, much of *The Crucible* is not fiction but fact. Arthur Miller carefully researched and dramatized events from the records of the Salem witch trials of 1692. These trials began in February of that year, and within seven months 20 people and two dogs had been killed for being witches. By the time the court was dismissed under various pressures, 55 people had confessed to being witches, and another 150 were accused and in jail. Most people, especially the Puritans, believed witches existed.

In light of these seemingly unbelievable events, Americans have long shown an interest in the Salem witch trials. But when *The Crucible* opened in January of 1953, audiences were not thinking only of Salem. At the time the country was actually gripped in its own "witch-hunt" hysteria. Senator Joseph McCarthy had charged in 1950 that 205 communists had infiltrated the state department, and with that accusation a national panic ensued that destroyed many Americans' reputations.

Arthur Miller himself was called before the House Un-American Activities Committee in 1956 and took the rather nonconformist path of testifying freely about his past association with communist groups. He refused, however, to name people he knew to be associated with such organizations.

Miller wrote in his biography, *Timebends,* that *The Crucible*'s theme of resistance to tyranny was its most important one. Relevant not only to the Salem witch trials and to the McCarthy hearings, this theme continues to be relevant; it is a part of humanity that will be wrestled with through the ages. We have Miller's thoughts while standing at Gallows Hill in Salem in 1953: "Here hung Rebecca, John Proctor, George Jacobs—people more real to me than the living can ever be. The sense of a terrible marvel again; that people could have such a belief in themselves and in the rightness of their consciences as to give their lives rather than say what they thought was false." Other timeless issues provoked by *The Crucible* are the individual's social responsibility; integrity and compromise; the power of guilt, love, conscience, fear, and hysteria; and adherence to supposedly religious principles.

The play is divided into four acts, and **Act I** opens with fear and tension. Young Betty Parris is in bed, alternately seemingly unconscious and then raving, and rumors have already spread that she has flown through the air. Her father, Reverend Parris, is more concerned about his social position and keeping his household from being charged with witchcraft than he is with his daughter's health or his congregation. We find out also that Parris saw his daughter with his niece Abigail dancing in the forest with his slave Tituba. This is a heinous sin for Puritans.

For a few moments when Betty, Abigail, and two other girls are left alone in the room, we find out that more than dancing went on in the woods. We learn that the girls were led in a conjuring ritual by Tituba, and that Mrs. Putnam had her daughter participate in an attempt to contact the souls of her seven dead infants. Abigail's evil was unleashed. In the woods she drank a blood charm in an effort to kill Elizabeth Proctor, her former employer. Now in the bedroom she violently shakes Betty, smacks her, and threatens her and the other girls if they dare say that anything other than dancing took place.

John Proctor, a well-respected farmer, enters the room looking for his servant, Mary Warren. He sends her home, and when he is alone with Abigail, she tells him that they danced in the woods; she laughs when he tells her that the town believes they practiced witchcraft. She reminds him of their sexual encounter, which he denies, and tells him that she longs for him.

Reverend Hale enters. A known expert on witchcraft, he lugs in many large, heavy books that he says are weighted with "authority." Proctor leaves, not wanting to get involved, but we will soon see how he is unable to maintain that stance, as much as he might like to.

Hale fiercely questions the girls. Abigail admits that she drank blood in the woods only because she was forced to by Tituba. Tituba admits to working with the devil, and finally, in an attempt to satisfy the inquisitor, the act comes to a frightening end, with Abigail, Tituba, and Betty frenziedly chanting lists of other women who are witches.

**Act II** begins some days later in the home of the Proctors, the only other private home we enter in the play. It quickly loses its privacy. The act opens with Elizabeth singing softly to the children upstairs, as her husband enters the house. He goes over to the fireplace and tastes the soup from the pot hanging there. This tranquility becomes strained, however, and trouble intensifies. Elizabeth Proctor greets her husband suspiciously, wondering why he is late. They talk of the madness in the village; she tries to convince him to tell the court that Abigail admitted to him that Betty's illness did not result from witchcraft.

The witch-hunt hysteria is infectious. More and more repectable people are accused. Mary Warren has been going to court against John Proctor's command. She reports that 39 women have been arrested and that Elizabeth herself was mentioned as a possible witch. Hale arrives and questions them about their Christian character. Ezekiel Cheever arrives next with a warrant for Elizabeth's arrest.

The second scene of Act II was added by Miller toward the end of the play's New York run, before it went on tour, but he later deleted it. The play has been performed both with it and without. Actor Laurence Olivier and numerous critics have seen it as unnecessary, although it does provide an expanded view of the play. In this scene, Proctor and Abigail meet in the woods at night. Proctor warns Abigail that he plans to expose her as a fraud: if need be, he will admit to their sexual indiscretion. She does not believe him and says she is happy that Elizabeth will die.

But in **Act III** John Proctor does bring Mary Warren to court, having convinced her to speak out against Abigail. Pressed by John, Mary says that she and the other girls have lied and that their afflictions in court were fake. Deputy Governor Danforth is disturbed, fearing personal attacks on his judgments and possible upheaval in the town if Mary is believed. He attempts to appease John Proctor by telling him that since his wife is pregnant, her life will be spared for a year.

By this time, though, Proctor has decided that he can no longer be concerned only with his own matters. As he upholds his plan to charge the girls with fraud, now in an attempt to free the accused wives of his friends, he is in full force, a formidable foe for Danforth. Abigail and the other girls are brought in for questioning, and Proctor insists that the court take Mary's signed statement against them. He accuses Abigail of plotting murder and reveals what she has told him about dancing in the woods. Following Abigail's lead, the girls act frightened of a force in the room that has inflicted a cold wind upon them. They shake and shiver and accuse Mary of controlling the wind. Proctor insists they are frauds. He admits that he has strayed sexually with Abigail, and that she told him her plans to dance on his wife's grave.

Elizabeth Proctor is brought in and asked if her husband is a lecher. She knows nothing about his confession, and she denies it, thinking that she is protecting him. Danforth decides that John has lied. In a further attempt to protect herself, Abigail cries out that Mary Warren has changed to a bird and is trying to tear at her face. She and all the girls run to one side, yelling and attempting to shield themselves. They let out a "gigantic scream," and succeed in wearing down the already crumpled Mary. She screams madly, continuing even after the other girls' cries have subdued. Proctor's attempts at supporting her are not enough. She turns on him, yells that he is in consort with the devil, and feeds Danforth's fears by crying that Proctor indeed intends to overthrow the court.

Proctor is thrown into jail. Hale storms out. He had begun to question the girls' testimony and fervently argue for fair appraisal, but his pleadings are far too late.

By **Act IV** we find that so many Salem residents have been jailed that the crops and cattle cannot be tended. People are protesting, and there have been disturbances in nearby Andover, where trials are also taking place.

Hale returns and tries to convince Danforth to pardon the well-respected people, especially Rebecca Nurse and John Proctor. When he realizes this is useless, he talks to Elizabeth Proctor, trying to persuade her to convince her husband to confess. Elizabeth talks to John. At first, for spite, John does not want to give in and confess. He asks his wife what he should do. She says that he must decide; whatever his decision is, she tells him, she will be behind it, for she knows "a good man does it."

John agrees to confess, but when told he must sign a written statement, he struggles, then signs it, then rips it up. He cannot add credence to the court's actions, and he cannot live his life with this lie. Shaken through this last act, he says of himself, ". . . for now I do think I see some shred of goodness in John Proctor." He is sent to the gallows. ❀

# List of Characters in
## *The Crucible*

**Reverend Samuel Parris** is a widower in his mid-forties who is more concerned about his reputation and what he deserves in his position than he is about the lives of his parishioners or his sick daughter. A repressive father and minister, he is insecure, vain, and paranoid, perfectly suited to support the authorities once the witch trials start.

**Betty Parris** is the minister's ten-year-old daughter, the focus at the play's beginning for having been caught dancing in the woods. She is one of the girls who creates disturbances during the main trial on stage.

**Thomas Putnam** is the wealthiest villager and a vindictive man. He is the community's strongest supporter of the trials, using them for personal vengeance.

**Tituba**, a native of Barbados, is the slave in the Parris household. She is the first accused of being a witch and blamed for Betty Parris's "illness."

**Abigail Williams** is Parris's seventeen-year-old orphaned niece who lives with him and Betty. She previously was employed by the Proctors, and while there she tempted John Proctor. Powerful and evil, she sees goodness as a sham and leads the girls in the commotion at the trial.

**Mary Warren** is the Proctor's 17-year-old servant. Initially sucked in by Abigail's strength, she later summons the courage to call the girls frauds in court, but then again succumbs to their evil pressures.

**John Proctor** is an independent-minded, well-respected Salem farmer in his mid-thirties. He is plagued with guilt and rage over a secret. Alternately labeled "very human" or "too good" by drama critics, no one denies that as the play progresses he is transformed.

**Reverend John Hale** is the recognized authority on witchcraft from a nearby town, laden down with books and enlightened too late.

**Elizabeth Proctor** is first presented as the aggrieved wife of John and later as loving and understanding. An upright community member, she is accused of being a witch.

**Judge Hathorne** is one of the judges sent to question the accused witches. In hindsight, Miller said he would have made this character even more evil.

**Deputy Governor Danforth** is a special judge sent to Salem. In his sixties and intent on upholding the power of the state at all costs, he is seduced by the girls' demonstration in court. ❁

# Critical Views on
## *The Crucible*

ERIC BENTLEY ON MILLER'S INNOCENCE

[Eric Bentley is a playwright and preeminent Brecht scholar. He has written a number of books, most recently *Bentley on Brecht* (1998). While in the following contemporary article he calls some of Miller's material magnificent, he believes *The Crucible* falls far short of the playwright's reputation.]

The first thing to say about Arthur Miller's *The Crucible* is that it is worth discussing, a fact that sets it off from all other English and American plays of the season. I found the occasion a moving one. To begin with, it is moving to see so many good American actors, or perhaps what I mean is that it's moving to see them permitted to act. Above all, at a moment when we are all being "investigated" or about to be "investigated," it is moving to see images of "investigation" before the footlights. It seems to me that there ought to be dozens of plays giving a critical account of the state of the nation, yet the fact of one such play, by an author who is neither an infant, a fool, or a swindler, is enough to bring tears to the eyes.

"Great stones they lay upon his chest until he plead aye or nay. They say he give them but two words. 'More weight,' he says, and died." Miller's material is magnificent for narrative, poetry, drama, meaning. The fact that we sense its magnificence suggests that either he or his actors have in part realized it, yet our moments of emotion only make us the more aware of half-hours of indifference or dissatisfaction. This is a story not quite told, a drama not realized. Pygmalion has labored hard at his statue but it has not come to life. There is a terrible inertness about this play. The individual characters, like the individual lines, lack all fluidity and therefore all grace. There is an O'Neill-like striving after a poetry and an eloquence which the author cannot achieve. "From Aeschylus to Arthur Miller," say the textbooks. The world has made this author important before he has made himself great; the reversal of the natural order of things weighs heavily upon him. It would be all too easy, script in hand, to point to weak spots. The inadequacy of particular lines, and characters, is of less interest, however, than the mentality from which they come. It is the mentality of the unreconstructed liberal.

There has been some debate as to whether this story of 17th century Salem "really" refers to our current "witch hunt" but since no one is interested in anything *but* this reference, I pass on to the real point at issue, which is: the validity of the parallel. It is true in that people today are being persecuted on quite chimerical grounds. It is untrue in that communism is not, to put it mildly, merely a chimera. The word communism is used to cover, first, the politics of Marx, second, the politics of Stalin, and, third, all the activities of liberals as they seem to illiberal illiterates. Since Miller's argument bears only on the third use of the word, its scope is limited. Indeed, the analogy between "red-baiting" and witch hunting can seem complete only to communists, for only to them is the menace of communism as fictitious as the menace of witches. The non-communist will look for certain reservations and provisos. In *The Crucible,* there are none. ⟨ . . . ⟩

The drama of indignation is melodramatic not so much because it paints its villains too black as because it paints its heroes too white. *Othello* is not a melodrama, because, though its villain is jet black, its hero's white radiance is not unstained. *The Crucible* is a melodrama because, though the hero has weaknesses, he has no faults. His innocence is unreal because it is total. His author has equipped him with what we might call Super-innocence, for the crime he is accused of not only hasn't been committed by him, it isn't even a possibility: it is the fiction of traffic with the devil.

—Eric Bentley, "Miller's Innocence," *New Republic* (February 16, 1953): pp. 22–23.

## HENRY POPKIN ON THE STRANGE ENCOUNTER

[Henry Popkin is a professor of English at the State University of New York at Buffalo and has produced an edition of Oscar Wilde's *The Importance of Being Earnest* (1965). In this extract he points out that Miller takes seriously only

Proctor and his wife, while he makes the witch-hunters and Abigail invincibly evil.]

*The Crucible*, too, turns upon a law which we should not respect: "Thou shalt not permit a witch to live." It takes the form of an investigation, for it begins with the arrival of the great investigator of witches. Our pursuit of the facts takes us over two paths; while the witch hunters make their efforts to measure the extent of witchcraft in the community, we follow John Proctor's attempt to weigh the guilt in his infidelity to his wife. The question of Proctor's guilt peters out since his guilt is nothing beside the community's. The issues are made a good deal simpler than those of the earlier plays. In our eyes, the community condemns itself, totally and without qualification, as it builds its airtight case against John Proctor. Contrasting his crime with the court's, the defendant justifiably thinks better of himself: "Now I do think I see some shred of goodness in John Proctor."

The play sustains considerable dramatic interest as the witch-hunters descend upon the Proctors, but it surely falls short in the realm of ideas—and especially by pressing so hard to make a particular judgment prevail. The actions of the witch-hunters are evidently to be attributed to the invincible evil of their characters. Notes to the printed version qualify this interpretation by strengthening the hints that these villains are motivated by greed, but Miller himself states that he did too much to mitigate the evil of the judge. At the same time, we require Proctor to be a model of good. Since we regard his adultery as a sin against his wife alone, he expiates it easily enough by sacrificing his life for hers. But Miller unintentionally reminds us how hard he is working to set up this adequate expiation for Proctor. Only Proctor and his wife are taken seriously. Abigail, who corrupted Proctor and now accuses his wife of witchcraft, could have been no more than seventeen when Proctor was her lover. She tells him he "put knowledge in her heart," and she continues to protest her love to him. But she is totally vile, she seduced him, he feels no obligation toward her, and evidently we are to regard her becoming a prostitute as a fitting result of her total depravity. Surely she needs more careful attention, and so does Proctor's responsibility toward her. Something is seriously at fault here. Miller no doubt began with the intention of creating an ulterior motive for the charges of witchcraft and also with the purpose of giving Proctor a less than mortal sin to expiate. But, giving his closest attention only to Proctor and to the main issue of the play, he lost sight of Abigail as a participant in a human relationship.

—Henry Popkin, "Arthur Miller: The Strange Encounter," *The Sewanee Review* 68, no. 1 (January–March 1960): pp. 41–42.

## Leonard Moss on the Portrayal of Hysteria, Honesty, and Their Consequences

[Leonard Moss is a former professor of comparative literature at State University of New York College in Geneseo. Here he points out the inconsistency between Miller's optimistic postscript to the play and its actual traumatic climax and sorrowful end.]

*The Crucible,* then, explores two contrary processes in the context of a given social order—the generation of hysteria and the achievement of moral honesty. How successfully are the two processes integrated? The first three acts are very well structured. Through an expository method Miller favored in earlier plays—delayed revelation of past sins—he reveals, in retrospect, that the central psycho-social issue of witchcraft arose from the private issue involving Abigail, John and Elizabeth Proctor—a Puritanical variant of the eternal triangle. ⟨ . . . ⟩ The second act, a transitional interlude bridging the introductory and climactic episodes, builds suspense and develops the two subjects preparatory to their simultaneous resolution in the trial scene. In the third act, Proctor and Hale cannot turn aside the forces maneuvered by Abigail, and the action ascends to its shrill emotional peak.

During this well-balanced ascent toward insanity, Proctor's personal difficulties are subordinate to Salem's ordeal. The conclusion abruptly reverses that relationship in a last-act shift of interest similar to, though not so disruptive as, the shift in *All My Sons.* Without warning, Miller's exhibition of devil-possession ceases. Having sparked Salem's "fire," Abigail disappears; "the legend has it that Abigail turned up later as a prostitute in Boston," a footnote explains.

Moreover, it seems that even as "terror" was spreading unchecked in Salem the condemnations were being called into question elsewhere in the area. The authority of the prosecutors has suddenly come to depend upon confession by those victims recently condemned, so that continued defiance by a highly regarded citizen like John Proctor will cure the town's fever. If Abigail's desire to supplant Elizabeth was the prime excitant of the madness, Proctor's desire to preserve his "name" becomes the prime depressant. When the protagonist realizes he cannot betray himself and his friends with a false confession, he at once completes his progression toward integrity and diverts Salem from its movement toward chaos.

The first consequence offers a consistent and positive, if unpleasant, denouement: facing execution in an irrational society, a man asserts his will to judge his own honesty and to oppose injustice. The second consequence, however, does not logically follow from the preceding action. ⟨ . . . ⟩ Nor can Proctor's last brave speeches, inspiring as they sound, account for the fact that after his hanging (Miller adds in a postscript) "the power of theocracy in Massachusetts was broken." How does Proctor's courage interrupt the "interior mechanism of confession and forgiveness"? What psychological impact does self-sacrifice have upon those who have triggered and those who have been crushed by that mechanism? The notion implied in the conclusion, that society may be redeemed by its maturest citizens, is an affirmative one. But this optimistic expectation, while intellectually gratifying, does not jibe with the traumatic agitation of the climax or with the quiet sorrow at the close.

—Leonard Moss, *Arthur Miller* (New York: Twayne, 1967): pp. 64–65, 66.

## ORM ÖVERLAND ON MILLER'S STRUGGLE WITH DRAMATIC FORM

[Orm Överland is a critic and translator. He has translated *Johan Schroder's Travels in Canada, 1863* (1989). In this piece he describes the lengths Miller goes to ensure that no point is missed.]

Miller's reluctance to let a play speak for itself became even more evident in his two attempts to add extra material to the original text of *The Crucible* after its first production in 1953. The first of these additions, a second scene in Act Two, helps to explain Abigail's behavior in Act Three, but, as Laurence Olivier told the playwright, it is not necessary. Although Abigail's psychotic character is brought out entirely in action and dialogue, in an encounter with John Proctor on the eve of the trial, and there is no suggestion of extra-dramatic exposition, the added scene is nevertheless evidence of Miller's sense of not having succeeded in making himself understood in the original version of the play.

More striking is the evidence provided by the series of non-dramatic interpolated passages in the first act, where the playwright takes on the roles of historian, novelist and literary critic, often all at once, speaking himself *ex cathedra* rather than through his characters *ex scena*. There is an obvious difference in intent as well as effect in writing an introductory essay to one's play and writing a series of comments that are incorporated in the text itself. The material used need not be different. For example, some of the comments on Danforth in the "Introduction" to the *Collected Plays* are quite similar to those on Parris or Hale incorporated in the play. In the one instance, however, he is looking at his play from the outside, as one of its many critics, in the other he has added new material to the play and has thus changed the text.

In effect the play has a narrator, not realized as a character but present as a voice commenting on the characters and the action and making clear some of the moral implications for the reader/audience. The director of the 1958 Off Broadway revival of *The Crucible* drew the consequences of the revised text and introduced "a narrator, called The Reader, to set the scenes and give the historical background of the play." Besides his function as one of the minor characters, this is what Alfieri does in *A View from the Bridge*. The introduction of a "narrator" element in *The Crucible* is closely related to Miller's attempts to have a separate voice present the author's view of the "generalized significance" of the "action" in the later play.

The interpolated expository passages of *The Crucible* serve two different purposes. Frequently the comments on a character merely repeat points made in that part of the drama which may be acted on the stage. Indeed, the opening words of the following paragraph on John Proctor are suggestive of the Victorian novelist guiding his readers through his story, making sure that no point, however obvious, may be missed:

> But as we shall see, the steady manner he displays does not spring from an untroubled soul. He is a sinner, a sinner not only against the moral fashion of the time, but against his own vision of decent conduct. These people had no ritual for the washing away of sins. It is another trait we inherited from them, and it has helped to discipline us as well as to breed hypocrisy among us. Proctor, respected and even feared in Salem, has come to regard himself as a kind of fraud. But no hint of this has yet appeared on the surface, and as he enters from the crowded parlor below it is a man in his prime we see, with a quiet confidence and an unexpressed, hidden force. Mary Warren, his servant, can barely speak for embarrassment and fear.

Proctor's sense of guilt is central to any understanding of him as a dramatic character, but certainly this is made sufficiently clear by, for instance, the several explicit remarks made by Elizabeth as well as by his behavior on the stage.

While such passages are further instances of Miller's apparent distrust of his medium as a means of communication, other passages speak of an impatience with the limitations of the dramatic form. Miller had researched this play thoroughly, and it is as if on second thought he has regretted that he had not been able to bring as much of his research and his historical insights into the play as he would have liked.

—Orm Överland. "The Action and Its Significance: Arthur Miller's Struggle with Dramatic Form," *Modern Drama* 18, no. 1 (March 1975): pp. 6–7.

## GERALD WEALES ON WHY THE PLAY IS NOT JUST ABOUT WITCH TRIALS AND MCCARTHYISM

[Gerald Weales is Professor Emeritus at the University of Pennsylvania. He is a drama specialist and reviewer and the author or editor of numerous titles, such as the Viking Critical Library edition of *Death of a Salesman, American Drama Since World War II* and *The Play and Its Parts*. In this extract, Weales explains the appeal of the play beyond its historical contexts.]

Does *The Crucible* portray the Salem witchcraft trials accurately? Does its use of Salem provide a workable analogy for the American political situation in the early 1950s? These are the two questions most often asked about *The Crucible*. ⟨ . . . ⟩ Anyone who goes to Arthur Miller to learn about Salem, to Bernard Shaw to learn about Saint Joan, to Peter Weiss to learn about either Marat or Sade is in trouble. A playwright may be drawn to a historical subject for any number of reasons, from the aesthetic assumption that a particular type of character can best be explored through a familiar figure, to the crassly commercial hope that a famous love story or a bloody battle will draw an audience. More often, among serious playwrights, the past is attractive as a means to saying something about the present. ⟨ . . . ⟩

The chief reason why Miller did not go for a one-to-one analogy between the Salem trials and the loyalty hearings of the 1950s is that beyond whatever immediate point he wanted to make as a political man he hoped, as an artist, to create a play that might outlast the moment. ⟨ . . . ⟩ Although my curiosity is strong enough to make me worry about what *The Crucible* has to say about Salem and Senator McCarthy, the questions that open this section of the introduction are not the kind that I ordinarily ask about a play. I want to know what it is, what it does, what it says right now. Interviewed in *Theatre World* in 1965, Miller said, "McCarthyism may have been the historical occasion of the play, not its theme." The important questions—at least, those about the play's meaning—should inquire into theme. What are the implications of John Proctor's final willingness of hang? of Danforth's need to hang him? of Elizabeth's acceptance of the death? of Parris's fear? of Hale's conversion? These are questions that do not depend on either of the play's historical contexts for an answer. Considered carefully, they may even explain the continued popularity of the play, its appeal to young men and women who have real or imagined Danforths of their own. ⟨ ... ⟩

Anyone with a touch of conscience, a hint of political interest, a whisper of moral concern will be drawn to *The Crucible*. Its big ideas are just right to set a classroom in motion, to turn it toward the kind of meaningful discussion which, in my youth, was called a bull session. Let the play carry you along, then, but stop now and then, for discipline's sake, and look at the details. Remember that Miller is a skilled playwright who can use the simplest incident for a multiple purpose. For example, look at the stewing rabbit at the beginning of Act II. The business in which Proctor tastes the rabbit, adds salt, and then compliments his wife on her seasoning lets us know that they have different tastes, that he is capable of at least a mild deception, and that he wants to please her. All that, with a pinch of salt.

A pinch? A grain, at least. That's how most generalizations should be taken.

—Gerald Weales, *Arthur Miller*'s The Crucible: *Text and Criticism* (New York: Penguin, 1977): pp. xiii–xiv, xv–xvi, xvii.

## ROBERT A. MARTIN ON *THE CRUCIBLE*'S BACKGROUND AND SOURCES

[Robert A. Martin is a professor of English at Michigan State University and co-editor of *The Theater Essays of Arthur Miller*. He has published numerous reviews and essays on American drama and literature. Here he explains Miller's diligence in using the actual record of the Salem witch trials. But Martin stresses that the play is not purely valuable as a political allegory.]

When *The Crucible* opened on January 22, 1953, the term "witch-hunt" was nearly synonymous in the public mind with the Congressional investigations then being conducted into allegedly subversive activities. Arthur Miller's plays have always been closely identified with contemporary issues, and to many observers the parallel between the witchcraft trials at Salem, Massachusetts in 1692 and the current Congressional hearings was the central issue of the play.

Miller has said that he could not have written *The Crucible* at any other time, a statement which reflects both his reaction to the McCarthy era and the creative process by which he finds his way to the thematic center of a play. If it is true, however, that a play cannot be successful in its own time unless it speaks to its own time, it is also true that a play cannot endure unless it speaks to new audiences in new times. The latter truism may apply particularly to *The Crucible,* which is presently being approached more and more frequently as a cultural and historical study rather than as a political allegory. ⟨ . . . ⟩

The events that eventually found their way into *The Crucible* are largely contained in the massive two volume record of the trials located in the Essex County Archives at Salem, Massachusetts, where Miller went to do his research. Although he has been careful to point out in a prefatory note that *The Crucible* is not history in the academic sense, a study of the play and its sources indicates that Miller did his research carefully and well. ⟨ . . . ⟩

Miller has said that if he were to rewrite *The Crucible,* he would make an open thematic issue of the evil he now believes to be represented by the Salem judges. His altered viewpoint toward the play may be accounted for partially as a reconsideration of his intensive examination of the trial records which, he has said, do not "reveal any mitigation of the unrelieved, straightforward, and absolute dedication to evil displayed by the judges of these trials and the prosecutors. After days of study it became quite incredible how perfect they were in this respect."

Miller's subsequent view of evil, however, did not come entirely from his study of the trial records. Between writing *The Crucible* in 1952 and producing the "Introduction" to the *Collected Plays* in 1957, he underwent a personal crucible when he appeared before the House Un-American Activities Committee in 1956. Although the experience was understandably not without its effect on his later attitude toward Congressional "witchhunters," it should, nevertheless, be considered in relation to his comments on the judges and evil quoted above. ⟨ . . . ⟩

Like the rock at Salem, *The Crucible* has endured beyond the immediate events of its own time. If it was originally seen as a political allegory, it is presently seen by contemporary audiences almost entirely as a distinguished American play by an equally distinguished American playwright. As one of the most frequently produced plays in the American theater, *The Crucible* has attained a life of its own; one that both interprets and defines the cultural and historical background of American society. Given the general lack of plays in the American theater that have seriously undertaken to explore the meaning and significance of the American past in relation to the present, *The Crucible* stands virtually alone as a dramatically coherent rendition of one of the most terrifying chapters in American history.

—Robert A. Martin, "Arthur Miller's *The Crucible:* Background and Sources," *Modern Drama* 20, no. 3 (September 1977): pp. 279, 280, 289–290.

## E. MILLER BUDICK ON HISTORY AND OTHER SPECTRES IN THE PLAY

[E. Miller Budick is a senior lecturer in the Departments of American Studies and English Literature at the Hebrew University of Jerusalem. He is the author of numerous critical works. In the piece that follows he focuses on Miller's consternation over a group's ability to create terror and impose their own "new subjective reality."]

Though *The Crucible* is, to be sure, unrelenting in its opposition to the authoritarian systems represented by Puritanism and McCarthyism, its use of historical materials and the position on moral tyranny which it thus projects seem to me far more complex than criticism on the play would suggest. For Miller's play is not interested only in proclaiming a moral verdict, either on historical or on contemporary events. It does not want simply to inculcate a moral by analogizing between past experiences, on which we have already reached a consensus, and contemporary problems, from which we may not have the distance to judge. Indeed, as Miller himself has stated, while "life does provide some sound analogies now and again, . . . I don't think they are any good on the stage. Before a play can be 'about' something else, it has to be about itself." Analogizing, then, is not, I think, either the major subject of the play or its major structural device. Rather, *The Crucible* is concerned, as Miller has claimed it is, with clarifying the "tragic process underlying the political manifestation," and, equally important, with describing the role of historical consciousness and memory in understanding and affecting such a process.

History is not simply a device which Miller employs in order to escape the unmediated closeness of contemporary events. Rather, it is a fully developed subject within the play itself. For history is for Miller precisely what enables us to resist the demon of moral absolutism. As Miller himself puts it:

> It was not only the rise of "McCarthyism" that moved me, but something which seemed much more weird and mysterious. It was the fact that a political, objective, knowledgeable campaign from the far Right was capable of creating not only a terror, but a new subjective reality, a veritable mystique which was gradually assuming even a holy resonance. . . . It was as though the whole country had been born anew, without a memory even of certain elemental decencies which a year or two earlier no one would have imagined could be altered, let alone forgotten.

It is this "subjective reality," and the problem of "memory," that are, I believe, at the heart of Miller's play. And for this reason Miller turns to the Puritan Americans for his subject. For the Salem witch trials raised supremely well the same terror of a "subjective reality" metamorphosing into a "holy resonance" and assuming an objective truth. Indeed, in one sense, this is what the controversy of spectre evidence was all about. Furthermore, the recreating of this "subjective reality" in the equally "subjective reality" of a drama representing both history and literature—themselves two versions of reality created by the human imagination—directly confronts the relationship of the subjective and the objective, and provides a model for mediating between the two, a model which has at its centre the very issue of memory which is also of paramount importance to Miller. Whether by intuition or by intention, "the playwriting part" of Miller digs down to the essential historical issues of the period as the historians themselves have defined them—issues such as spectral evidence, innate depravity, and its paradoxical corollary, visible sanctity—and relates these issues to the problem of human imagination and will.

Like so much historical fiction and drama, *The Crucible* forces a revolution in our perception and definition of reality. It causes what appears to us to be immediate and real—the present—to become dreamlike and subjective, while it enables what we assume to be the less stable aspects of our knowledge—the ghosts of the past—to assume a solidity they do not normally possess.

—E. Miller Budick, "History and Other Spectres in Arthur Miller's *The Crucible*," *Modern Drama* 28, no. 4 (December 1985): pp. 535–537.

## Wendy Schissel on A Feminist Reading

[Wendy Schissel is Co-President of St. Peter's College in Muenster, Saskatchewan, an affiliate college of the University of Saskatchewan. She teaches English and Women and Gender Studies. She is the author of *The Keepers of Memory: Canadian Mythopoeic Poets and Magic Realist Painters* (1992). Here she questions Miller's and critics' treatment of the play's female characters.]

Arthur Miller's *The Crucible* is a disturbing work, not only because of the obvious moral dilemma that is irresolutely solved by John Proctor's death, but also because of the treatment that Abigail and Elizabeth receive at Miller's hands and at the hands of critics. In forty years of criticism very little has been said about the ways in which *The Crucible* reinforces stereotypes of *femme fatales* and cold and unforgiving wives in order to assert apparently universal virtues. It is a morality play based upon a questionable androcentric morality. Like Proctor, *The Crucible* "[roars] down" Elizabeth, making her concede a fault which is not hers but of Miller's making: "It needs a cold wife to prompt lechery," she admits in her final meeting with her husband. Critics have seen John as a "tragically heroic common man," hu*manly* tempted, "a just man in a universe gone mad," but they have never given Elizabeth similar consideration, nor have they deconstructed the phallologocentric sanctions implicit in Miller's account of Abigail's fate, Elizabeth's confession, and John's temptation and death. As a feminist reader of the 1990s, I am troubled by the unrecognized fallout from the existential hu*man*ism that Miller and his critics have held dear. *The Crucible* is in need of an/Other reading, one that reveals the assumptions of the text, the author, and the reader/critic who "is part of the shared consciousness created by the [play]." It is time to reveal the vicarious enjoyment that Miller and his critics have found in a cathartic male character who has enacted their sexual and political fantasies.

The setting of *The Crucible* is a favoured starting point in an analysis of the play. Puritan New England of 1692 may indeed have had its parallels to McCarthy's America of 1952, but there is more to the paranoia than xenophobia—of Natives and Communists, respectively. Implicit in Puritan theology, in Miller's version of the Salem witch trials, and all too frequent in the society which has produced Miller's critics is gynecophobia—fear and distrust of women. ⟨ ... ⟩

It would be foolish to argue that John does not suffer—that, after all, is the point of the play. But what of Elizabeth's suffering? She is about to lose her husband, her children are without parents, she is sure to be condemned to death as well. Miller must, once again, diminish the threat that Elizabeth offers to John's martyrdom, for he has created a woman who does not lie, who her husband believes would not give the court the admission of guilt "if tongs of fire were singeing" her. Miller's play about the life and death struggle for a *man's* soul, cannot be threatened by a woman's struggle. In order to control his character, *Miller* impregnates her. The court will not sentence an unborn child, so Elizabeth does not have to make a choice. Were she to choose to die without wavering in her decision, as both John and Miller think she would, she would be a threat to the outcome of the play and the sympathy which is supposed to accrue to John. Were she to make the decision to live, for the reasons which Reverend Hale stresses, that "Life, woman, life is God's most precious gift; no principle, however glorious, may justify the taking of it," she would undermine existential integrity with compromise.

—Wendy Schissel, "Re(dis)covering the Witches in Arthur Miller's *The Crucible:* A Feminist Reading," *Modern Drama* 37, no. 3 (Fall 1994): pp. 461, 469.

[Stephen Marino completed a doctorate at Fordham University. He teaches and leads creative writing workshops at St. Francis College in Brooklyn. In this criticism, Marino explores Miller's use of "weight" to reinforce his perspectives on man's struggle for truth.]

One of the more intriguing historical events Arthur Miller included in *The Crucible* was Giles Corey's refusal to answer his indictment for witchcraft in order to preserve his land for his sons' inheritance. In punishment, Corey was pressed with great stones, still refusing to confess to witchery. Corey died, still in defiance, uttering his last words, "More Weight." Miller assigns great significance to Corey's words for he uses them in Act Four at a decisive moment for his protagonist, John Proctor. In hearing about Giles's death, Proctor repeats Corey's words, as if to consider their meaning for himself. In fact, Miller intimately connects the word "weight" to the theme of the play by employing it ten times throughout the four acts. Tracing the repetition "weight" in *The Crucible* reveals how the word supports one of the play's crucial themes: how an individual's struggle for truth often conflicts with society. ⟨ . . . ⟩

Miller's thematic use of weight is intimately connected to the conflicts that occur when an individual's struggle to know truth opposes society's understanding of it. For the dramatic tension of the play is based on the clashes of truth between those characters who profess to speak it, those who profess it, those who live it and those who die for it.

Miller's initial use of "weight" in the first scene immediately connects it with truth. Reverend Parris, trying to discover the cause of his daughter Betty's unnatural sleeping fit, pleads with, and then threatens, his niece Abigail:

> Now tell me true, Abigail. And I pray you feel the weight of truth upon you, for now my ministry's at stake, my ministry and perhaps your cousin's life.

The "weight of truth" Parris implores Abigail to consider operates on a number of levels both in this scene and in the rest of the play. Obviously, Parris wants to discover the literal truth about the abominations that Abigail, Betty, and the other girls, led by Tituba, are alleged to have performed in the forest. However, the "weight of truth" which Parris begs Abigail to consider more importantly encompasses all of its figurative meanings: seriousness, heaviness, gravity, importance, burden, pressure, influence—all of which are connected to religion and law, the foundations upon which the theocracy of Salem village is built. For clearly *The Crucible* questions the meaning of truth in this theocratic society and the weight that that truth bears on an individual and on the society itself.

Thus, Parris's appeal to Abigail to "feel the weight of truth" contains many thematic implications. On one level, Parris's use of weight as "importance" or "seriousness" appeals to Abigail on a personal level, since her uncle's ministry and her cousin's life are at stake. On another level, because Parris invokes his ministry in connection with the "weight of truth," the religious connotation is clear. If Abigail felt the weight of religious truth, she would confess to Parris about the abominations performed in the forest, thereby releasing her from the heaviness of falsehood, sin, guilt, and the power of Satan. On another level, Miller clearly establishes negative connotations of the "weight of truth." For there is no doubt that Parris threatens Abigail with all the heaviness of his ministry, and the severe power of theocracy that it represents for Abigail and the inhabitants of Salem village—a power whose weight and truth we see unleashed in the play.

—Stephen Marino, "Arthur Miller's 'Weight of Truth' in *The Crucible*," *Modern Drama* 38, no. 4 (Winter 1995): pp. 488–490.

# Works by
# Arthur Miller

*Situation Normal.* 1944.

*Focus.* 1945.

*All My Sons.* 1947.

*Death of a Salesman: Certain Private Conversations in Two Acts and a Requiem.* 1949.

*An Enemy of the People* by Henrik Ibsen (adaptor). 1951.

*The Crucible.* 1953.

*A View from the Bridge (with A Memory of Two Mondays): Two One-Act Plays.* 1955.

*Collected Plays.* Two volumes. 1957, 1981.

*The Misfits.* 1961.

*Jane's Blanket.* 1963.

*After the Fall.* 1964.

*Incident at Vichy.* 1965.

*I Don't Need You Any More: Stories.* (as *The Misfits and Other Stories*) 1967, 1987.

*The Price.* 1968.

*In Russia* (with Inge Morath). 1969.

*The Portable Arthur Miller.* Ed. Harold Clurman, 1971. Ed. Christopher Bigsby, 1995.

*The Creation of the World and Other Business.* 1973.

*In the Country* (with Inge Morath). 1977.

*The Theater Essays of Arthur Miller.* Ed. Robert A. Martin. 1978.

*Chinese Encounter* (with Inge Morath). 1979.

*Eight Plays.* 1981.

*Playing for Time: A Screenplay.* 1981.

*The American Clock.* 1982.

*Elegy for a Lady.* 1982.

*Some Kind of Love Story.* 1983.

Salesman *in Beijing.* 1984.

*The Archbishop's Ceiling.* 1984.

*Two-Way Mirror: A Double Bill (Elegy for a Lady* and *Some Kind of Love Story).* 1984.

*Up from Paradise.* 1984.

*Playing for Time: A Full-Length Stage Play.* 1985.

*Danger: Memory! (I Can't Remember Anything* and *Clara).* 1986.

*Timebends: A Life.* 1987.

*Conversations with Arthur Miller.* Ed. Matthew C. Roudane. 1987.

*Plays: One.* 1988.

*Plays: Two.* 1988.

*The Archbisop's Ceiling; The American Clock.* 1988.

*The Golden Years and the Man Who Had All the Luck.* 1989.

*Early Plays.* 1989.

*On Censorship and Laughter.* 1990.

*Plays: Three.* 1990.

*Everybody Wins: A Screenplay.* 1990.

*The Last Yankee.* (one-scene version) 1991; (two-scene version) 1993.

*The Ride Down Mount Morgan.* 1991.

*Homely Girl: A Life* (with Louis Bourgeois). Two volumes. 1992.

*Arthur Miller in Conversation.* Steven R. Centola. 1993.

*Broken Glass.* 1994.

*The Last Yankee; with a New Essay About Theatre Language; and Broken Glass.* 1994.

*Plays: Four.* 1994.

*The Theater Essays of Arthur Miller* (revised and expanded). Ed. Robert A. Martin and Steven R. Centola. 1996.

*Mr. Peters' Connections.* 1998.

# Works about
# Arthur Miller

Adam, Julie. *Versions of Heroism in Modern American Drama: Redefinitions by Miller, Williams, O'Neill, and Anderson.* New York: St. Martin's Press, 1991.

Bentley, Eric. "On the Waterfront." In *What Is Theatre?* New York: Beacon, 1956, pp. 98–102.

Bergeron, David M. "Arthur Miller's *The Crucible* and Nathaniel Hawthorne: Some Parallels," *English Journal* 58 (1969): pp. 47–55.

Bhatia, Santosh K. *Arthur Miller: Social Drama as Tragedy.* New Delhi: Arnold-Heinemann, 1985.

Bigsby, C. W. E., ed. *File on Miller.* London: Methuen, 1988.

Bloom, Harold, ed. *Arthur Miller.* New York: Chelsea House, 1987.

_____, ed. *Arthur Miller's The Crucible.* Philadelphia: Chelsea House, 1999.

_____, ed. *Arthur Miller's Death of a Salesman.* New York: Chelsea House, 1988.

_____, ed. *Willy Loman.* New York: Chelsea House, 1990.

Bonnet, Jean M. "Society vs. the Individual in Arthur Miller's *The Crucible*," *English Studies* 63 (1982): pp. 32–36.

Brucher, Richard T. "Willy Loman and the Soul of a New Machine: Technology and the Common Man." *Journal of American Studies* 17 (1983): pp. 325–36.

Brustein, Robert. "Arthur Miller's Mea Culpa." *The New Republic* (February 8, 1964): pp. 26–30.

Calarco, N. Joseph. "Production as Criticism: Miller's *The Crucible*." *Educational Theatre Journal* 29 (1977): pp. 354–61.

Carson, Neil. *Arthur Miller.* New York: Grove Press, 1982: pp. 60–76.

Choudhuri, A. D. "*Death of a Salesman:* A Salesman's Illusion." In *The Face of Illusion in American Drama,* ed. A. D. Choudhuri. Atlantic Highlands, N.J.: Humanities Press, 1979, pp. 94–111.

Clurman, Harold. "Arthur Miller." In *Lies Like Truth*. New York: Grove, 1958, pp. 64–72.

Cohn, Ruby. "The Articulate Victims of Arthur Miller." In *Dialogue in American Drama*. Bloomington: Indiana University Press, 1971, pp. 68–96.

DelFattore, Joan. "Fueling the Fire of Hell: A Reply to Censors of *The Crucible*." In *Censored Books: Critical Viewpoints*, ed. Nicholas Karolides, et al. Metuchen, N.J.: Scarecrow Press, 1993.

Ditsky, John. "Stone, Fire, and Light: Approaches to *The Crucible*," *North Dakota Quarterly* 46:2 (1978): pp. 65–72.

Dukore, Bernard F. *Death of a Salesman and The Crucible*. Atlantic Highlands, N.J.: Humanities Press, 1989.

Elsinger, Chester. "Focus on Arthur Miller's *Death of a Salesman:* The Wrong Dreams." In *American Dreams, American Nightmares*, ed. David Madden. Carbondale: Southern Illinois University Press, 1970, pp. 165–74.

Ferres, John H., ed. *Twentieth Century Interpretations of The Crucible*. Englewood Cliffs: Prentice-Hall, 1972.

Flaxman, Seymour L. "The Debt of Williams and Miller to Ibsen and Strindberg," *Comparative Literature Studies*, Special Advance Issue (1963): pp. 51–59.

Ganz, Arthur. "The Silence of Arthur Miller." *Drama Survey* 3 (1963): pp. 224–37.

Harder, Harry. "*Death of a Salesman:* An American Classic." In *Censored Books: Critical Viewpoints*, ed. Nicholas J. Karolides, Lee Burress, and John M. Kean. Metuchen, N.J.: Scarecrow Press, 1993, pp. 209–19.

Hayman, Ronald. *Arthur Miller*. New York: Ungar, 1972.

Jackson, Esther M. "D*eath of a Salesman:* Tragic Myth in the Modern Theatre," *CLA Journal* VII (September 1963): pp. 63–76.

Koon, Helen Wickham, ed. *Death of a Salesman: A Collection of Critical Essays*. Englewood Cliffs, N.J.: Prentice-Hall, 1983.

Lahr, John. "Birth of a Salesman." *The New Yorker* (December 25, 1996): pp. 110–113.

Mander, John. "Arthur Miller's *Death of a Salesman.*" In *The Writer and Commitment.* Philadelphia: Dufour, 1962, pp. 138–52.

Martin, Robert A., ed. *Arthur Miller: New Perspectives.* Englewood Cliffs: N.J. Prentice-Hall, 1982.

McMahon, Helen. "Arthur Miller's Common Man: The Problem of the Realistic and the Mythic." *Drama and Theatre* 10 (1972): pp. 128–33.

Meserve, Walter J., ed. *The Merrill Studies in Death of a Salesman.* Columbus: Merrill, 1972.

Miller, Jeanne-Marie A. "Odets, Miller, and Communism." *CLA Journal* 19 (1976): pp. 484–93.

Nathan, George Jean. "The Crucible," *Theatre Arts* 37 (April 1953): pp. 24–26.

O'Neal, Michael J. "History, Myth, and Name Magic in Arthur Miller's *The Crucible.*" *CLIO* 12, no. 2 (Winter 1983): pp. 111–22.

Partridge, C. J. "*The Crucible.*" Oxford: Basil Blackwell, 1971.

Popkin, Henry. "Arthur Miller's *The Crucible,*" *College English* 26 (November 1964): p. 141.

Porter, Thomas E. "The Long Shadow of the Law: *The Crucible.*" In *Myth and Modern Drama.* Detroit: Wayne State University Press, 1969, pp. 177–99.

Prudhoe, John. "Arthur Miller and the Tradition of Tragedy." *English Studies* 43 (1962): pp. 430–39

de Schweinitz, George. "*Death of a Salesman:* A Note on Epic and Tragedy," *Western Humanities Review* XIV (1960): pp. 91–96.

Shaw, Patrick. "The Ironic Characterization of Bernard in *Death of a Salesman.*" *Notes on Contemporary Literature* 11, no. 3 (1981): p. 12.

Tynan, Kenneth. *Curtains.* New York: Atheneum, 1961.

Welland, Dennis. "Two Early Plays," *Miller: A Study of His Plays.* London: Eyre Methuen, 1979.

# Index of
# Themes and Ideas